The Answer

Why not use Allan Pease as guest speaker for your next conference or seminar?

Allan and Barbara Pease are the most successful relationship authors in the business. They have written a total of eighteen bestsellers – including ten number ones – and give seminars in up to thirty countries each year. Their books are available in over one hundred countries, are translated into fifty-five languages and have sold over 27 million copies. They appear regularly in the media worldwide and their work has been the subject of nine television series, four stage plays and a number-one box-office movie, which attracted a combined audience of over 100 million.

Their company, Pease International Ltd, produces videos, training courses and seminars for business and governments worldwide. Their monthly relationship column was read by over 20 million people in twenty-five countries. They have six children and eight grandkids and are based in Australia.

The Answer

How to take charge of your life & become the person you want to be

Allan & Barbara Pease

This edition first published in Great Britain in 2017 by Orion
an imprint of the Orion Publishing Group Ltd
Carmelite House, 50 Victoria Embankment,
London, EC4Y 0DZ
An Hachette UK Company

1 3 5 7 9 10 8 6 4 2

A CIP catalogue record for this book
is available from the British Library.

Trade Paperback ISBN: 978 1 4091 6828 7

Illustrations by John Hepworth

Printed in Great Britain by Clays Ltd, St Ives plc

MIX
Paper from
responsible sources
FSC® C104740

Note: While every effort has been made to ensure that the information in this book is correct, it should not be substituted for medical
advice. Neither the publisher nor the authors accept any legal responsibility for any personal injury or other damage or loss arising from
the use or misuse of the information in the book.

Every effort has been made to fulfil requirements with regard to
reproducing copyright material. The author and publisher will be
glad to rectify any omissions at the earliest opportunity.

We dedicate The Answer *to Ray Pease,*
whose knowledge, experience and influence
touched everyone who knew him.
His wisdom pervades the pages of this book.

Contents

Acknowledgements

Here is a partial list of some of the people who have knowingly or unknowingly contributed to some of our concepts, ideas and stories. Professor Susan Greenfield, Dr David Buss, Darrin Cassidy, Ray and Ruth Pease, Bill and Beat Suter, Anthony Robbins, Brian Tracy, Dr Gennady Polonsky, Kath McConnell, Vicky Cook, Jim Cathcart, Jack Canfield, Loren Wimhurst, Raelene Boyle, John Fenton, Tony Earle, Dr Helen Fisher, John Hepworth, Dr Henning Kukenrenken, Dr Patch Adams, Professor Alan Garner, The Junipers, Dorie Simmonds, Glenda Leonard, Gerry Hatton, Rita Hartney, Jerry Seinfeld, Grant Sexton, Anatoly Sobchak, Dr James Moir, Dr Mark Bowman, Dr Denis Waitley, Professor Phillip Stricker, Fiona Hedger.

Introduction

> 'Life should not be a journey to the grave with the intention of arriving safely in a pretty and well-preserved body, but rather to skid in broadside in a cloud of smoke, thoroughly used up, totally worn out, and loudly proclaiming "Wow! What a Ride!"'
> **Hunter S. Thompson**

Picking up *The Answer* is the first step in taking yourself down roads you may never have considered before and may not even have known about. By the time you are halfway through reading it, you will realise why you are where you are, and why you have what you have at this point in your life. You will have the answers that will help take you to wherever you are capable of going.

In *The Answer*, we will show you how to decide what you really want out of life and how to get it. You'll learn how to prioritise your ideas, reclaim your life, deal with obstacles, and avoid being manipulated by others, especially friends and family members. We'll help you to choose your own path, not one that someone tries to push you down. We will show you how to take charge of your life and become the person you want to be. You will discover how to deal with any circumstances that arise, no matter how difficult, overwhelming or hopeless they may seem when they first appear.

You will learn how to go from where you are now to where

you'd like to be. We will show you the proven principles of success that men and women have used throughout history to achieve greatness and to recover from, or overcome, failure. Barbara and I learned many of these principles directly from some of the masters over the past 50 years, and these lessons are the main motivation for our own personal successes. We will also explain new studies of the brain that reveal why some people are hugely successful while others aren't. We will explore a brain-operating system that you can program to take you anywhere you want to go. Starting with Giuseppe Moruzzi and H. W. Magoun, scientists have discovered a part of the brain that directs and determines the level of success or failure that each of us has in our lives. We will discuss this brain system in the first chapter, and the benefits that come from using it will form the basis of everything we cover throughout the book.

Also, we will answer your questions about anything you have ever read or heard about goal-setting, visualisation, affirmations, prayer, alpha thinking and the Law of Attraction. As there is so much information throughout the book, we encourage you to put it down to reflect on and implement what has been said. We have suggested points at which to do this, indicated by the ᕼ symbol. This does not need to be strictly followed and is only a guide.

We will discuss the simple but powerful skills we have learned that help us deal with almost everything that happens in life – good or bad. And we'll answer the big questions about how to get anything you want from life, despite what can sometimes seem like impossible circumstances.

The concepts we will explore here have changed the lives of the participants in our seminars, and they can change your life too. This book is called *The Answer* because that's what you'll find in it.

So if life is a game, these are the rules.

Many key points are repeated in several forms throughout the book, and this is intentional. Studies show that the most effective learning occurs with spaced repetition of an idea in a series of six exposures. The first time you hear or read a statement your mind can reject it because it may conflict with your preconceived ideas. This is why most motivational training doesn't work. When you have heard the same idea six times, your brain can accept it and internalise it.

We have provided activities in each chapter and encourage you to write directly in the book, for ease and to use as a reference point if you would like to return to the text.

Finally, in case you're wondering, while *The Answer* is co-authored by both of us, it is largely written in the first person as Allan, to make it easier to read.

Allan and Barbara Pease

Chapter 1

Revealing the Secret of the RAS

**'Whatever the mind can conceive and believe,
the body can achieve.'
Napoleon Hill, 1937**

When Napoleon Hill made this landmark statement in 1937 in his classic book *Think and Grow Rich*, he didn't have the medical science, brain scanners or technology we now take for granted to prove his beliefs. He claimed that if you could think clearly of something and you really wanted it, you could achieve it. Science has removed much of the mystery and hocus pocus surrounding iconic statements such as Hill's, and we now have scientific insights into the processes of achievement, goal-setting, self-fulfilling prophesies, the function of prayer and the Law of Attraction. Science can now show us where and how success works in the brain. You are about to learn about a remarkable system we each have in our brains – the **Reticular Activating System**, or **RAS**.

The RAS, located in the brain stem of the mammalian brain, is a bunch of neural fibres commonly known as the Reticular Formation. The RAS plays a part in many important functions in human biology, including sleeping and waking, breathing, the beating of your heart and behavioural motivation. The RAS also contributes to sexual arousal, appetite and eating, the elimination of body waste, control of consciousness and the ability to bring certain things to your attention. Trauma to the RAS can cause a coma and has been linked to several medical conditions, including narcolepsy.

The RAS functions as a network of neurons and neural fibres running through the brain stem, and these neurons connect to various other parts of the brain. This system has two parts: the ascending RAS, which connects to parts of the brain including the cortex, the thalamus and the hypothalamus; and the descending RAS, which connects to the cerebellum and to nerves responsible for the various senses.

THE RETICULAR ACTIVATING SYSTEM

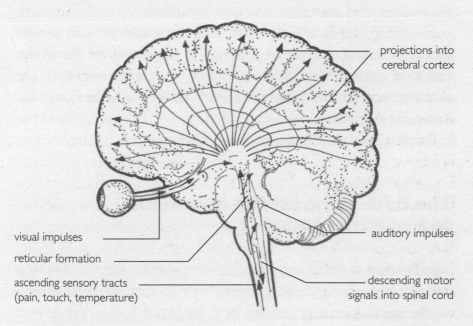

projections into cerebral cortex

visual impulses

reticular formation

ascending sensory tracts
(pain, touch, temperature)

auditory impulses

descending motor
signals into spinal cord

By the mid-20th century, physiologists had proposed that some structure deep within the brain controlled mental wakefulness, alertness and motivation.

Scientists first became aware of the existence of the RAS in 1949 when, at the University of Pisa, H. W. Magoun and Giuseppe Moruzzi investigated the neural components regulating the brain's sleep–wake mechanisms and reported their findings in the inaugural volume of the scientific journal *Electrocephalography and Clinical Neurophysiology*. This early research eventually led to the discovery that the RAS is the portal through which nearly all information enters the brain (smells are the exception: they go directly into the brain's emotional area). The RAS filters the incoming information and affects what you notice, your level of arousal, and decides which information is not going to get access to your brain.

The RAS is connected to the spinal cord at its base, from

where it accepts information that comes directly from the ascending sensory tracts. Any new information or learning must enter the brain through one or more of the senses and is decoded by the sense-specific receptors of the body. From there the information travels through the nerves in the skin or body to the spinal cord and up through the Reticular Activating System to the part of the brain that receives input from that particular sense.

The RAS is the brain's command and control centre

The RAS is a place where your thoughts, internal feelings and the outside influences meet. It produces dynamic effects on the motor activity centres in your brain and in the cortex activity, such as the frontal lobes. It is a network of nerve pathways that filter all the sensory input your brain receives from your external world. Whatever you see, hear, feel or taste passes through the RAS. Put simply, the RAS is the key to switching on your brain and is the brain's main centre of motivation.

How the RAS works
The brain processes over 400 million bits of information every second but only 2,000 bits can be processed consciously. The remainder is processed without your awareness. In other words, 99.9999 per cent of the information presented to you every day goes unnoticed. This is the only way we can deal with everyday life and the millions of bits of information flooding into our awareness and demanding our attention. If you had to deal with all the messages simultaneously, you would not be able to cope and would pass out. So evolution

has given us the RAS – the equipment with which to filter all information and to extract only what is important to us at any given moment.

Your RAS functions like a sorting office, evaluating the incoming information and prioritising that information in the form of messages that need your attention. It's a filter between your conscious and subconscious mind, and it takes instructions from your conscious mind and passes them on to your subconscious. Your brain then instructs your body to make the physical actions necessary to comply with the image the RAS instructs. It sorts through your environment for information patterns that best match your beliefs or the things that are familiar to you. Then it links your thoughts and feelings with similar things in your environment. When it finds a match, your conscious mind is alerted.

Variations of the RAS

The RAS also exists in other primates. Chimpanzees, for example, share 99 per cent of our DNA and, like a human's, a chimp's RAS receives all incoming sensory data. It scans and prioritises that data in accordance with its hardwired 'programs', just as it does in humans. It controls the chimp's basic functions of pulse, sleep, awareness, digestion and cardio-vascular function, as it does in humans. Where its function differs from that of humans is that we have a more highly developed sense of 'self'. We are driven by an insatiable need to know who, what, why, where and when. A chimp's RAS operates like a primitive computer that runs basic programs; a human RAS functions like the latest, most dynamic computer system.

In the brains of some people, the RAS can't always efficiently excite the cortex as it should. Such people have difficulty learning, poor memory and little self-control.

When the RAS is overstimulated, our behaviour is marked by hyper-vigilance, sensory hypersensitivity, constant talking, restlessness and hyperactivity. For people diagnosed with attention deficit disorders (ADD and ADHD), the ascending RAS does not have enough of the chemical norepinephrine to excite the cortex. Norepinephrine is the same chemical that is released whenever our heart rate increases, or our breathing hastens, and so on. People with ADD/ADHD can take drugs that temporarily make the RAS more efficient at using the norepinephrine it already has. This helps their concentration, their perception, their ability to memorise and improves their learning.

The RAS also deals with social contacts. Introverts have more activity going on in their RAS than extroverts. Scientists believe that the RAS of an introvert is aroused more easily than that of an extrovert because introverts often have difficulty talking to others, and when they do, their brains show a strong reaction, similar to a type of panic.

The RAS has a GPS and a search engine
Your RAS responds to your name, to anything that threatens your survival, and to information that you need to know immediately. For example, if you're looking for a computer file that you're sure you placed somewhere on your desktop, your RAS alerts your brain to search for the name of the file – say, an overseas travel itinerary – or it will focus on one word in the filename to help you find it. The function of the RAS is also what is often commonly called the Law of Attraction.

**'Marcus Aurelius said, "Man becomes what
he thinks about all day long."
If that was true, I'd be a woman.'
Steve Martin**

Your RAS has a built-in GPS system. With a GPS, you don't need to know where all the roads are located in a given city. You only need to decide *where* you want to go. You input the data and the GPS directs you. If you take a wrong turn, it puts you back on track. The satellite software in a GPS works out how to get you there – and that is *exactly* how your RAS works. With a GPS you need to decide *where* you want to go, not *how* you will get there. In exactly the same way, once you've decided your goal, your RAS begins to see everything connected with it. If you veer off-course, it reroutes you. More on this later.

The RAS is also similar to a heat-seeking missile – you put in the co-ordinates of where you want it to go, press the launch button and it goes there. On the way, it filters out all the useless information around you and only keeps what's relevant. For example, the instruction might be 'Listen for my name', so if you are walking through a busy shopping mall or airport and your name is called over the PA system, you'll hear it.

**The RAS works the same way as
a heat-seeking missile.**

How your belief system works

Scientists have found that the RAS also controls our belief system and it will only recognise or select information that supports our beliefs. This means that, no matter what we believe or think, our RAS will pay more attention to it or will filter all other information around us to help us to get to what we have chosen to believe. This is why some people see opportunities whereas others see difficulties. It is also why some can believe things that the rest of us know not to be true.

In the Chinese language, the word 'crisis' is composed of two characters, one representing danger and the other opportunity.

It is obvious that how you feel about any event is influenced by what you think it means. In other words, your belief system will determine whether your RAS will work for or against you. If you believe that you can only make money by working harder, you'll only see information that confirms this belief and you'll proceed in life as if this were true. Your RAS will filter out any opportunities that offer you ways to make more money without having to work harder.

Your RAS can either work for you or against you. It depends entirely on what you think about.

If you want your RAS to work for you, then you must program it to watch out for what you want, not for what you don't want. When you program a specific idea or a goal into your RAS, it doesn't matter whether you're asleep or awake, or whether you're thinking about it or not – the RAS will find precisely what you've told it to find, just like the search function on a computer. It will pick out the relevant data from the millions of bits of information around you for your attention and it will edit out irrelevant information. When you create a clear, focused picture of what you want, the RAS kicks into high gear and doesn't stop until it finds it for you. We'll explore this in more detail later.

How the RAS chooses which information it will see

Imagine that you're walking through a busy, noisy airport terminal. Think of all the sounds that surround you – hundreds of people talking, music and announcements. You can hear the general background noise, but your RAS does not listen to each individual sound. Let's say that an announcement comes over the PA, saying your name or maybe your flight number. Suddenly, your attention is at its peak because your RAS brings this relevant information to your immediate, conscious attention. Your RAS acts as a filter, dampening the effect of all the other repeated stimuli, such as the loud noises, and prevents your senses from being overloaded. Then it brings your name forward.

Why you see your car everywhere

Have you ever noticed that once you have decided on the type of car you want to buy, it seems that every other car on the road is the one you are considering buying? You also see it in car parks, on TV and at shopping malls. That car is everywhere. This is because your RAS is working, filtering out the other cars (the unimportant information) and bringing the car of your thoughts to the forefront of your mind. The numbers of that particular car have not increased since you decided to buy it; it's simply your RAS in action. If you lose interest in that car, you'll no longer see it on the roads.

Your RAS is why you see your car everywhere you go.

When a woman becomes pregnant, it starts to seem to her as if every second woman around her is also pregnant. If you have a new baby in the house you may be so tired that you can sleep through the noise of the traffic and noisy neighbours, but as soon as the baby begins to cry you are wide awake.

In a very different example, if you choose to believe that the world and people are all bad, every time you turn on the TV or read a newspaper you'll see tragedy, death and war. The RAS doesn't care whether you love something or not, it only looks out for the patterns in your environment that match your dominant thoughts or beliefs.

If you are continually thinking about what you don't like, then your RAS is being programmed to alert you to see what you don't like. You will see so much of what you don't want that it could seem as though you are at war with your environment. **This is why we will ask you to focus only on what you do want, not what you don't want.**

Summary

It turns out that Napoleon Hill was right – and now we have the science to prove it. You program your RAS with your self-talk and expectations. If your expectations are positive, you automatically program your RAS to seek information about positive behaviours and to screen out information about negative ones. Because of this biological filter function, whatever you are thinking about or focusing on will seep into your subconscious mind and reappear at a future time.

The exciting breakthrough is that you can deliberately program your RAS by choosing the exact messages you send to it from your conscious mind. This means you can now create your own reality. Nothing you will learn in this book is connected to willpower. It all happens in this small bunch of neural fibres running through your brain stem – your Reticular Activating System – your RAS.

In the following chapters you will learn how to program it.

**'...there is nothing either good or bad,
but thinking makes it so.'
Shakespeare**

Chapter 2

Decide What You Want

A boat docked in a tiny Mexican village. An American tourist complimented the Mexican fisherman on the high quality of his fish and asked how long it took him to catch them.

'Not very long,' answered the fisherman.

'*Then why didn't you stay out longer and catch more?*' *asked the American.*

The fisherman explained that his small catch was sufficient to meet his needs and those of his family. The American asked, 'But what do you do with the rest of your time?'

'*I sleep late, fish a little, play with my children, and take a siesta with my wife. In the evenings I go into the village to see my friends, have a few drinks, play the guitar, and sing a few songs...I have a full life.*'

The American interrupted. 'I have an MBA from Harvard and I can help you! You should start by fishing longer every day. You can then sell the extra fish you catch. With the increased revenue, you can buy a bigger boat. With the extra money the larger boat will bring, you can buy a second one and a third one and so on until you have an entire fleet of trawlers. Instead of selling your fish to a middleman, you can negotiate directly with the processing plants and maybe even open your own plant. You can then leave this little village and move to Mexico City, Los Angeles, or even New York City! From there you can direct your huge enterprise.'

'*How long would that take?*' *asked the fisherman.*

'*Twenty, perhaps twenty-five years,*' *replied the American.*

'*And after that?*' *asked the fisherman.*

'*Well, that's when it gets really interesting,*' *answered the American, laughing. 'When your business gets really big, you can start selling stocks and make millions!*'

'*Millions? Really? And after that?*'

'*After that you'll be able to retire, live in a tiny village near the coast, sleep late, play with your children, catch a few fish, take a siesta with your wife, and spend your evenings drinking, singing, playing the guitar and enjoying your friends!*'

Do you have a secret ambition to achieve something great? If you do, how long will it remain a secret? Most people never discover what they really want to do with their lives. As you will soon read, most people do not like going to work, most people who live to old age are broke and most people are killed by something such as cancer, heart disease and other physical illnesses. Hardly anyone dies of old age. This chapter will show you the first dilemma most people struggle with – how to decide what you want. At first this may sound simple – to decide what you want from life – but most people don't have a process for figuring out how to do it.

The reason most people don't accomplish much or have much in their lives is because they haven't decided what they want.

Most people struggle with questions such as 'How do you define success?'; 'Who do I want to become?'; 'What do I want to experience?'; 'What assets do I want to accumulate?'

Everyone knows the feeling of having an inner urge to do something that excites you whenever you think of it. But generally, people rarely make that thing happen.

Why most people never do much

When you were born you were absolutely clear on what you wanted in life and you refused to let anyone or anything stand in your way of getting to it. If you were hungry you cried loudly until someone fed you. When you could crawl you fearlessly headed for the door, a toy or a pet you wanted and no-one was going to stop you. By the time you could talk you were hammering your parents over and over with your wants until they either gave in to you or *they* ran away from home. Overall, you laughed at most things that happened in life and didn't take yourself too seriously. So what happened between childhood and adulthood?

Well, when most kids were young, their RAS was being continually programmed with phrases such as:

Act your age – grow up
You should be ashamed
You are selfish
Accept what you've been given
Who do you think you are?
No, you don't feel like that
Eat everything on your plate
I wish you were more like…
You are a bad child!
Don't say that!
Because I'm your mother, that's why!
If everyone jumped off a bridge would you do it too?
Because I said so
I'll teach you the meaning of the word 'No!'
Do what I say – not what I do
You're just like your useless father/mother
Money doesn't grow on trees
Don't pull that face, the wind will change and you'll be stuck
  like that
Wear clean underwear in case you're in an accident
Stop crying or I'll give you something to cry about
Be grateful for what you have and don't keep wanting more
There are children starving in Africa
This is going to hurt me more than it's going to hurt you

As a result of this RAS conditioning, most people arrive at puberty being compliant to the demands of others. The spontaneity and dreams they had as children have been suppressed or completely lost. By their late teens they are doing things that adults want them to do and, whether they realise it or not, have been conditioned into making choices such as marrying the 'right' person rather than someone they want to marry, they take university courses that their parents want them to take, or they choose a 'secure' job instead pursuing an exciting life. They take the safe, 'sensible' path in life and many then tiptoe silently through life to retirement and early death.

A TRUE STORY – ROBERT

Robert's father had reprimanded him all his life to 'Do the right thing and stop being so selfish.' As a teenager living in Europe, Robert dreamed of being an artist and wanted a career in social work, helping underprivileged people. His father told him that would be a waste of time and that Robert could never support a family doing it. He wanted Robert to be a doctor – not because the income potential was better, but because he wanted to brag to his friends that his son was a doctor. Robert's father sent him to New Zealand and paid for all his accommodation and university fees. After seven years of diligent study, which Robert didn't like much, he qualified as a microbiologist, and, to his father's joy, soon became a medical doctor.

As we are writing this story, Robert is teaching abseiling in New Zealand. He spends his time in child education and is taking art classes. He has no intention of returning to his home in Europe. He will never work as a medical doctor and doesn't care much if he never sees his father again.

Robert went to New Zealand to get away from his dominating father but he still fulfilled his father's dream of becoming a doctor because his father footed the bills. The price Robert paid was seven years of his life and a failed relationship with his father. Was it all worth it?

What's the point of climbing the ladder of success to discover you've leaned it against the wrong wall?

Living up to others' expectations is futile and will only bring you anxiety and unhappiness. We respect people who are passionate about what they want and who beat their own drum, even when we don't necessarily agree with what they might want in life. Make a decision now that you will take control and do what you want in life, not what others may demand of you.

How to decide *what* you want

The starting point is to write down anything you think you may want to do or achieve, regardless of how trivial it may seem to anyone else. Include on your list any dreams you had as a child that still hold some significance for you. Also, record any idea you may see or hear about that strikes a chord with you. Try to have at least ten to twenty items on this list and include anything that has ever seemed appealing to you. And we mean *anything*. Writing something on a list doesn't mean you are committed to it; it's just an idea that appeals to you right now or has interested you at some point in the past. When you start your list, keep it to yourself or share it only with someone you completely trust. Do not discuss the list with anyone who may want to manipulate you or tell you that something on your list is a silly idea or can't be done. This list is all about *you*. Do not show it to dream-stealers and never allow yourself to be defined by someone else's opinion.

**Don't let people who gave up on their
dreams talk you out of yours.**

Decide *what* – not *how*

Most people don't get the things they want in life because
they focus on **how** they might achieve something. They look
at what others have achieved and think, *I wouldn't know how
to do that*. So they do nothing. Instead they should decide
what they want to achieve.

The first and most important principle in achieving any
goal is to decide what you think you might want. Don't
think about how you will achieve it. Your RAS will do that
for you.

As you now know, your RAS has a built-in GPS system,
so you only need to decide where you want to go and it will
take you there.

If you concentrate on how something *could* be done, you
can become discouraged because, right now, you either
don't know a way of doing it or you don't have the skills or
circumstances that are required to achieve it. And so nothing
happens – you never get started. The most important lesson
right now is to think about **what** you want and don't, **under
any circumstances**, think about **how** you will do it – not yet.
We'll get to this later.

Let's repeat this: Think first only about **what** you want. Do
not consider **how** you'll do it. Not yet. For now, just write
down the '**what**'. Use your RAS.

First decide *what* you want. Your RAS will then search for the answers to the question of *how* to achieve it and the ways will begin to appear.

Create a goals book

Collect pictures, images and text that describe or illustrate your goals. Put them in a book, and read it every day. As an example, here are some of the things Barbara and I have written on our personal lists. Some items we wrote together, others we wrote individually, and some at different times in our lives.

Achieve these goals

Run a marathon
Live on the beach
Build a lake
Achieve a black belt in martial arts
Parachute jump
Have own TV show
Head a big company
Be a well-known speaker
Fly on Concorde
Give a seminar in Russia
Be a stage hypnotist
Catch a snake by hand
Float in the Dead Sea
Write and record a Top-40 record
Live in a castle

Earn a bronze medal in life-saving
Catch a funnelweb spider
Win a surfing competition
Bungee-jump
Travel to 50 countries
Join a gym
Climb the Pyramids
Write a bestselling book
Represent Australia in basketball
Be famous on TV
Be a top salesperson
Live in a foreign country
Play guitar in a rock band
Have my own business
Be a millionaire by age 30
Own a Mercedes Benz

Learn how to

Tap-dance
Ride a skateboard
Scuba-dive
Ride a horse
Ski
Read music
Give massages
Speak French and German
Speed-read
Write music
Sing in tune
Take great photographs
Perform magic
Raise smart kids

Box
Be an outstanding parent
Be a helicopter pilot
Be a publisher
Be an expert in health
Sail
Dance rock and roll
Raise positive, health-conscious kids
Be a strong swimmer
Moonwalk
Meditate
Cook Japanese food
Write four-part harmonies

Learn to play

Lead guitar
Piano
Drums
Saxophone
Bass guitar
Violin
Harmonica

These lists are wide and varied and include things that often just seemed like an interesting idea at the time. But, either individually or together, we have started and mostly achieved over 90 per cent of the items we wrote on these lists. Some we achieved at a world-class level, for others we received national acclaim or awards; some were on a local level, and some were only significant to us personally. And some we were really crap at – Barbara no longer wants to play the piano and I don't want to tap-dance any more. A few goals have not been completed yet and some were abandoned because, once we got into them, we discovered that we didn't really like them.

'The secret of getting ahead is getting started.'
Mark Twain

Why writing a list works

Have you ever noticed that when you read a newspaper or magazine, you see some articles but not others? You may feel that you've read everything in that paper until someone asks if you read a particular article and you can't recall seeing it. You then reread the paper and discover that the article fills an entire page! But you didn't see it. This is because your RAS is a target-seeking mechanism that only lets you see things related to the thoughts and ideas you've put into it. For example, if you constantly think about sports but never about flower arrangements, you'll constantly see articles written about sports and sportspeople in newspapers or magazines but you won't see anything about flower arrangements, even though these articles were also there.

Your RAS only seeks out things relative to what has been programmed into it and ignores the rest. If, for example, you decide to think only about tigers, everywhere you look you'll see stories, movies and information about tigers. You'll see tigers on the television, on the Internet, in magazines, on cereal packets and on advertising billboards, and you'll hear people talking about tigers. Yet prior to deciding to think about tigers, you probably never saw anything about them.

**When you write an item on your list you will
begin to see information about it everywhere.**

As I've said, the same thing happens when you buy a car. If, for example, you decided to buy a white, four-door Toyota, you'd begin to see them everywhere – on the motorways, in car parks, on TV, in dealers' forecourts and in people's garages. But before you decided to buy the white Toyota, you probably never noticed them.

Whatever car you drive, you see others driving it everywhere you go. You can't stop seeing your car. It's all around you. That's why whenever you write a goal, the information and answers about it begin to appear in front of you. In other words, your RAS makes it materialise.

The Spaghetti Principle

Your thoughts and ideas are like a ball of spaghetti in your head. One thought is intertwined with many others, so it becomes difficult to separate a single idea and focus on it. Writing your ideas on paper is important because writing crystallises each thought so that it can be considered in isolation to the others. Then, as you read your written list and think about the items on it, some items that may have seemed important at the start might lose their lustre, while others that might have originally seemed minor can begin to stand out as more exciting.

As an example, when I was a kid I saw Gene Kelly's movie *Singing in the Rain* and I loved the way Kelly could flawlessly tap-dance around a room. By my twenties, I had seen the movie several times and decided I would love to learn to tap-dance like him. I wrote it on my list and it stayed there for about five years. But as soon as I had written it down as a possibility I began to see tap-dancers in the movies and on TV; articles about tap-dancing started to jump out at me from everywhere. These TV shows and media about tap-dancing had always been there but I hadn't noticed them until I wrote it on my list. At age 35, I joined a tap-dancing class. More on that later.

Why handwriting your list is so important

Psychology professor Dr Gail Matthews, at Dominican University in California, ran a study on goal-setting with 267 participants. She found that you are 42 per cent more likely to achieve your goals just by handwriting them. When you use a keyboard to type, it only involves eight different movements of your fingers and this uses only a small number of neural connections in your brain. Handwriting can involve a range of up to 10,000 movements and creates thousands of neural paths in your brain. This explains why handwriting has much greater impact on your emotional attachment to your goals and on your commitment to them. Using a computer to record your goals is certainly helpful, but this is like reading a text about how exciting it is to own a sports car. Handwriting your goals is like your brain taking the sports car on a test drive through the Alps. You become more emotionally involved and it dramatically heightens your motivation to achieve that goal. Writing your goals activates your RAS and instructs your subconscious to work on them, whether you are thinking about them or not.

In the 1980s, the idea of giving seminars behind the 'Iron Curtain' in Russia (the USSR) was considered impossible. Westerners, generally, couldn't go to Russia at that time.

But Barb and I put this on our list anyway, because it sounded like an exciting idea and had a James Bond feel about it. As soon as we wrote it down, we immediately began to see information, newspaper articles, TV documentaries and magazine stories about Russia appearing everywhere around us. Today, as a result of writing this on our list in 1989, Russian-speaking countries have become some of our biggest publishing and seminar markets. If we had decided that the Russian idea was just a crazy thought, and hadn't written it down, Russia would never have become a major business destination for us because the RAS would not have searched for information on the *how*. This is why it's so important that you don't think about *how* to get what you want.

When you decide exactly *what* you want to do, have or become, your RAS will begin to seek out the ways to do it. Once you put the thought into your mind, you'll begin to see, read and hear things about it. It's that simple. And this is what very few people ever do.

Constantly rereading your written list of goals will soon clarify how important or unimportant each item *really* is to you. Keep adding to your list, modifying it, and subtracting from it. After a while, some of the items will keep reappearing on it because these are the ones that will have the most meaning for you. Put your list on your bedroom or bathroom wall, put another copy on your refrigerator or use it as a screen saver on your computer or mobile device. Put a copy in any location where you can always see it. As you think of new things, add them to the list. The longer your list, the better.

The difference between millionaires and billionaires

A study of wealthy people in the 1970s was conducted to determine the main differences between millionaires and billionaires. While both groups were wealthy, the researchers wanted to know why one group was so dramatically wealthier than the other. After three years of research, the one point that was the most similar between the two was that both groups knew exactly what they wanted. But the billionaires had clearly written lists of their ideas, goals and objectives. Surprisingly for the researchers, the existence of a written list of intentions was the most striking difference. While the millionaires were equally passionate about their goals and knew exactly what they wanted, they had a significantly lower incidence of written plans than did the billionaires. In another USA study of goal-setting, Paul J. Meyer reported that:

3 per cent of people in the USA had definite, written goals and plans
10 per cent had a good idea about their life goals
60 per cent had considered their goals but only related their finances
27 per cent had given little thought to goal-setting or their future.

Of the people in this study, Meyer reported:

3 per cent were highly successful
10 per cent were moderately well off
60 per cent were described as of 'modest means'
27 per cent were barely getting by with help or charity.

The message here is clear. Make a list of your goals – in handwriting.

How to discover your true career path or life mission

How you spend your working life is usually one of the top priorities on most people's lists, yet studies show that more than eight out of ten people don't like what they do for a living. A Gallup poll in 2012, covering 140 countries, showed that 67 per cent of people are 'not engaged' in their work – or are simply not motivated and are unlikely to exert extra effort – while another 24 per cent are 'actively disengaged' or truly unhappy and unproductive.

Do you look forward to waking up on a workday? Do you get out of bed every morning excited about the possibilities of what could happen that day? If not – and there's at least an 80 per cent chance that's the case – then what should you be doing with your work life?

Here is the answer to finding your life's mission – what is it in your past that you enjoyed doing more than anything, and that you loved so much that you'd do it for free if given the opportunity? Think back to the things in your life that gave you the most joy and happiness, and made you feel the best. These are the areas in which you will find your life's mission or true career.

**Ask yourself, 'What is the one thing that
I would love to do so much that I'd do it for free,
but that I could also get paid for?'
When you can answer this question you have
discovered one of your life's missions.**

Many people don't consider that they can make a great living or become rich by doing what they love. But if you write it on your list, you will find the way. You may say, 'I love socialising with people and talking. How can I do that for a living?' Well, Jay Leno, David Letterman, Michael Parkinson and Oprah Winfrey loved that too. Maybe you think, I really love making my home a beautiful place to be. Well, so did Martha Stewart. 'I really love to play sport'... think of Tiger Woods, Roger Federer, Pat Rafter and Greg Norman. Sure, these people have become wildly successful and mega-rich in their pursuits, but each began as an unknown person who pursued the thing they loved to do the most and would do it for free. Think of the tens of thousands of others who are not famous but who make a successful living out of these same pursuits. Remember, the expert in anything was once a beginner.

**Find something you love to do and you
will never work another day in your life.**

Maybe you enjoy eating out at nice restaurants, reading books and magazines, going to parties and dance clubs, watching movies, listening to or playing music, meeting new people, surfing the net, playing sports and shopping. Well, thousands of people get paid to do those things. It's okay to love eating out and to claim that food is your passion. But why not write a goal to start your own restaurant, or a restaurant review website or a newsletter, blog or magazine, or become a chef? If you enjoy listening to music you might also enjoy producing your own music or covering the music industry as a journalist on your own blog. By producing things for other people to enjoy or use in their lives you convert a passion into a sustainable income.

The things you are passionate about are not random. They are your calling. When I was at school I loved being a stand-up comedian and telling jokes. One of my teachers once said I should pursue a career as a 'professional smartass'. And that's exactly what I have done for over 40 years. I never knew how I'd do it – I just decided to do it and my RAS did the rest. By age 24, I had written a training program about how to sell. And it sold like hot cakes! I then decided to write a bestselling book and become an author. I didn't know how to do this or what the book would be about but, importantly, I decided to just do it, despite having only gone to year 11 in school, despite the fact that English was my worst subject. I was just going to do it – period. As soon as I wrote the goal I began to see answers as to how to do it. Two years later, I decided that a book about how to read other people could be a hit. So I sat down and wrote the first line – 'Once upon a time...' The first line is always the hardest, but this line got me started. I titled it 'The Language of the Customer's Body'. At age 27, I published it as my first major book, which I finally called *Body Language*. The rest is history.

You can make a great living out of doing anything that really turns you on. But first you need to decide exactly what you love and then write it down.

From today, we want you to stop thinking in terms of getting a 'job'. A 'job' can be an interim way to pay the bills while you are chasing your passion. A 'job' is something a person does when they'd rather be doing something else. And this applies to over 80 per cent of people. When we asked what you would do for free if you could, did you reply by saying you would still do your current job? If you gave another answer, then start planning right now to **get out of the job you are in.**

The definition of a 'job' – Just Over Broke.

Millions of people are making successful careers right now from the things that turn them on. They wake up every day full of excitement about going to do more of it. This is what you need to do too, if you want to live a fulfilling life. Starting in a venture or career purely to make money does not stand the test of time, and it can make you cynical and unhappy. Do what your heart says you were meant to do and the money will eventually follow.

Don't be pushed by your problems.
Be led by your dreams.

Summary

Start writing a list today of anything in life you find interesting or exciting. Don't judge the things on your list; just write them down. If you see a billboard advertising bungee-jumping (as Barbara and I did) – write it down. If you watch fabulous rock 'n' roll dancing on TV (which I did) or watch a story about someone living in a foreign castle (as Barbara did) – write it all down. By learning how to activate your RAS, which is part of your cortical arousal system, you increase your chances of being more efficient in achieving your goals.

By writing down your goals you learn to focus your attention on what really matters. Doing this gets your RAS aroused and working in your favour. When you write your goals, you crystallise your thinking and pinpoint the destinations that you want to move toward. Your RAS will locate the exact steps needed to get there.

The most successful people in life write their thoughts down and prioritise their ideas. As soon as their thoughts are on paper, their RAS begins to source the answers to achieving what they want.

Reclaim your life today and don't take the path that someone tries to push you down, regardless of how honourable this person's intentions may seem.

- Decide right now to take charge of your own life and to reclaim yourself.
- Decide now to have what you want and to become the person you want to be.
- If you are not working every day on something that excites you, plan to get out of it. Studies show that most people

don't like what they do for a living. Don't be one of them.
- Start writing your list now. Not later, or after breakfast, or after reading this book. Do it **now**. Otherwise, one day you will wake up to discover you are out of time.

_____
_____
_____
_____
_____
_____
_____
_____
_____
_____
_____
_____
_____
_____
_____
_____
_____

**You'll never leave where you are until
you decide where you'd rather be.**

Chapter 3

Set Clearly Defined Goals

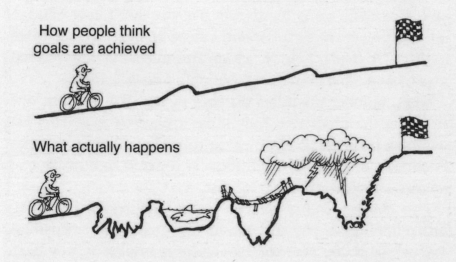

How people think goals are achieved

What actually happens

People are motivated by one of 2 things – to receive a benefit or to avoid a loss. Some goals can have elements of both. For example, you may want to reach a senior level in your company to gain prestige and more money to provide things for your family while, at the same time, you also want to avoid the pain of not having enough resources to provide for your loved ones.

Humans are motivated to either make a gain or avoid a pain.

Now that you have written your master list, this chapter will show you how to begin turning your ideas into realities.

Rewrite all your list items under three sections with the headings – **A, B & C**. Items marked 'A' are things you are sure you would like to achieve soon or are things that seem most significant to you right now. Items marked 'B' also seem significant to you right now but you'll need some more time to think about each before you consider making any commitment to them. The 'C' items are things you feel might be fun or challenging to attempt but you don't have enough information yet to be sufficiently motivated to upgrade them to 'B' or 'A' items. Your 'C' items are interesting or appealing ideas, but at this point, they are only possibilities.

Next, number the items on your **A** and **B** lists from one to ten in the order that they most appeal to you. This list will now form the basis of where your life will go from now. Prioritise your list now and look at it again tomorrow and rewrite as necessary.

This chapter will show you how to achieve a wide and different range of physical and mental goals in your business and personal life. Also we'll give you examples of how Barb and I reached some of our own goals using the principles you have read about so far.

As previously mentioned, some were accomplished on a private level, some on a local level, some at a state or national levels and others, globally. For example, we had five books in the European Bestseller list at one time and were the world's most successful non-fiction authors. We were entered into the *Guinness Book of Records*, we learned to dance rock 'n' roll, lived in a castle, I can moonwalk and Barbara has bungee-jumped into a ravine. In a later chapter we'll show you how we achieved some of these results and why it's remarkably simple – not easy – but simple. This chapter

A

_____

_____

_____

_____

_____

_____

_____

B

_____

_____

_____

_____

_____

_____

C

_____

_____

_____

_____

_____

_____

_____

will show you how simply you can do things that – to many people – can seem amazing or impossible.

Quantifying your goals

A goal is anything that you personally feel motivated about or would like to achieve, based on your own personal value system. For some people that may mean power or money, for others it could be finding a cure for cancer or helping the starving people in Africa. It's whatever motivates you personally.

For a goal to be motivational it must be stated in clear, measurable terms with specific dates, times, amounts, shapes, colours, dimensions and outcomes. For example, if you were to say your goal was 'to be rich one day', this lacks motivational power because it's not a clear target to shoot at – it's too generic and vague and your RAS can't get a handle on it. If however, you stated it this way: 'By 12 p.m. on 15 August, 5 years from today, I will have $1 million of net assets and will be completely debt-free' then you will feel motivated to take immediate action because you have specific amounts, times and deadlines and your RAS will go into 'search mode'.

If your goal was 'to own a nice home', for example, you will not develop the motivation to achieve this because 'a nice home' is a vague concept. A billionaire might view his house as a 'nice home' in the same way a Botswanan bushman sees his grass hut in the desert as 'a nice home'. If, however, your goal was 'to own a 4 bedroom brick home with a tropical garden, facing Northeast, 100 meters from the beach in a warm climate, 3 years from today', then your RAS will be activated to immediately start searching for the 'how' to achieve it. When you can clearly describe the floor plan, landscaping, furniture, door handles, building materials, bench tops and floor surfaces, your RAS will begin to imagine what it would feel like to live there. When a house is advertised for sale that meets that specification, your RAS will bring it to your attention. You then go to visit it, experience its atmosphere, absorb the smell and feel of it and collect brochures about it. The more measurable and quantifiable you make the goal, the more driven your RAS will be to reach it.

Your goal should be out of reach but not out of sight.

If you are not satisfied with your current progress in life, it's because your goals are not clearly defined enough for your RAS to know where to search. When your goals become crystallised into fine detail and you know where you are today and where you want to go, your RAS fires up and motivation occurs.

State your goals in the positive

People often state their goals in negative terms. The RAS, however, can only see positive images – it can't picture something that is not there. This is why negatively framed goals are rarely achieved. For example, a smoker who decides to quit could state their goal like this: 'I will quit smoking by January 1.' But a smoker's brain already has strong, positive images of the smoker smoking cigarettes. To say that you *won't* do something is to ask your RAS to imagine something that it can't visualise, and the RAS can't do that. If you were to write it like this – 'By 1 January, I will be a non-smoker' – your RAS can form an image of what a *non-smoker* looks like. It can visualize you with clean fingernails, fresh breath, white teeth and a healthy appearance. It will bring to your attention toothpaste advertisements, people exercising and images of how confident and popular you are becoming.

Positively stated goals create motivational images in the mind whereas negatively stated goals create no mental images at all.

That's why, if you weigh 100 kilos and want to lose 10 kilos, stating, 'I will lose 10 kilos' won't work. Your mind already has a clear picture of you at 100 kilos and this image demands that you eat enough to maintain that size. However, stating, 'By 20 June I will weigh 90 kilos' you let your mind picture what you will look like at that weight and this instructs your RAS to match that image. The RAS will pass this 90 kilo image on to your subconscious and it will drive you toward this goal.

State your goals so that your mind can see positive images – do not try to force it to imagine things that can't be seen.

'If you want a happy life, tie it to a goal, not to people or things.'
Albert Einstein

Make your goals tangible

Have you ever taken a test drive in a new car then experienced getting back into your old car? You would have felt dissatisfied and would become even more motivated to push harder toward your goal of owning a new car. The closer you are physically and emotionally to the images connected to your goals, the faster you will reach them. For example, if you wanted to have a red, four-seater convertible you would search for images, reviews, sales data and brochures about that car. But if you take a test drive in it along the coastline (where your beach house will be), the experience will heighten all the feelings and emotions associated with this goal.

If you want to give back to society you can feel inspired by reading stories about others who did the same. But if you volunteer to help out in a Salvation Army soup kitchen for a night or spend a day assisting the underprivileged, you'll have a wild hunger to do more if it's really a right goal for you. If you want to send your kids to the top schools, book a school tour and experience it first-hand – don't just read about it. Don't think about how you will pay for the school fees, let your RAS figure it out. Most people meet their life partners by accident. Finding the right life partner is one of the most significant events in most of our lives, so why not search for exactly what you want in a person? If your image of the perfect life partner is, for example, an athletic, bright, positive-thinking, blue-eyed blonde (as it was in my case), only date people who fit that criteria. Most people don't do this. They make their choices from whatever – or whoever – shows up in their lives or on dating sites.

**Only write goals for what
you really want. Don't settle for
the best of only what you can see.**

How your brain deals with goals

If you can't imagine it, then you don't have what is required
to be able to achieve it right now. Your brain will only visualise the things that you are physically or mentally capable of
achieving. The sports world has understood this concept for
decades – if you can picture yourself reaching a particular
goal, your body can do it. Erin Shackell and Lionel Standing
of Bishop's University even demonstrated that if you mentally
practise lifting weights, your body will respond to those
images and alter your body to give over 80 per cent of the
result you'd achieve if you actually lifted the weights!

For example, if you can imagine yourself becoming prime
minister or president of your country, it means that you have
the necessary fundamentals somewhere within you to do this or
you wouldn't be capable of imagining it in the first place. So if
you can write this on your list, it means you have it within you
to achieve this goal, no matter how daunting it may seem at
first. This presents exciting opportunities – if you can think
about something, your body can achieve it! Just as Napoleon
Hill said in 1937.

**If you can imagine it, you
have it in you to do it.**

If you can picture yourself being a multi-millionaire, you have it within you to do it. If you can see yourself bungee-jumping into a raging river, your body can do it. If you can imagine yourself confidently addressing an audience of 20,000 people, then you have the right stuff in you somewhere to do it. If you can imagine yourself as being healthy and disease-free, your body will work toward that outcome. Life offers no guarantees that you can have all these outcomes, but being able to first visualise a situation puts you on the track that can lead to its achievement. The most important first step is to first imagine yourself *achieving* the result and not to think about **how** you'll do it. We'll discuss the **how** soon. And this is what most people don't do – they try to imagine **how** to do something and then give up on the idea, frustrated.

'In the absence of clearly defined goals we become strangely loyal to performing daily trivia until we become enslaved by it.'
Robert Heinlein, Science Fiction Writer

Your RAS in action

When you have set a goal that you are passionate about, your RAS will focus your mind. You suddenly become aware of things that you may not have paid any attention to in the past, but are now useful or important to you. For example, your goal would be easier to reach if you could meet the right people. At a business function or party you hear a person's name mentioned, a person who has the connections that would help you move your goal forward. In the past your RAS would have ignored the name because it was of no use to you, but when it's relevant to a goal you want to achieve it suddenly becomes important. So you make a point of introducing yourself to this person and the connection is made. Your RAS filtered that piece of information in a fraction of a second because it was activated when you decided what was important to you. Even though the event was noisy and the music was loud, your RAS was able to filter that specific piece of information.

Put your goals lists everywhere

Display your written list of goals everywhere: on your refrigerator, as a screen saver on your computer, phone – everywhere. This forces your brain to constantly evaluate each goal then it will decide how significant it really is to you. This also lets your brain rehearse how your life will be when you actually achieve each goal. The brain has over 3 billion electrical connections that instruct your body to obey its instructions. That's why, when you can clearly picture yourself achieving your goal, your RAS instructs your brain cells to direct your body to complete your mental image and that's why putting your lists up everywhere around you works so well.

Cut out pictures or print images of everything connected with your goals. Images of homes, vacations, cars, bungee-jumping, speaking in front of large crowds, saving the universe and so on. Have a page featuring all these images or buy a blank book to keep as your current goals book.

Between Barbara and I, we have (so far) listed over 200 goals in our joint lives and have completed 122 of them to date, including building 3 lakes, giving seminars in the Kremlin, living in a castle and writing 10 number 1 bestsellers. And we wrote all our goals in lists in a book.

Life begins at the end of your comfort zone

If you upgrade a goal from your C list to your B list – or from B to A – and that goal no longer seems to have the same lustre you thought it had, you can either downgrade it, alter it or remove it from your list and find something new. When you have a list of goals, modifying or eliminating one item is not a big deal. People who only have one goal often stick with it even when it's no longer important or relevant to them and may even be failing.

A TRUE STORY – HANK

The idea of climbing to the top of Uluru, the ancient, giant red rock near Alice Springs in Central Australia, appealed to me (Allan) so I wrote it on my C list. I thought I would probably like to do it within the next 5 years but even if I didn't do it by then, it would still stay on my master list for later. I thought only about what I wanted to do – climb the rock – and not how I'd do it. As soon as I had written it down I began seeing news articles and documentaries about Uluru everywhere – I wasn't searching for them, they just kept appearing. About 3 years later, I was sitting in a coffee shop when, above all the other noise, I heard two people having a conversation at the next table about a conference that was being held at Uluru. I jumped into the conversation immediately, found out about the conference, made some phone calls and sold myself onto the program as a speaker. Six months later, I climbed Uluru. Goal achieved!

About a year later, I was speaking at a conference about goal

Me standing on top of Uluru

setting and I mentioned how I got to climb Uluru. A delegate, Hank — an electrician — asked, 'How does this apply to me, Allan? I'd like to climb Uluru too. But because you're in the conference business it was easier for you to get to go there. I'd have to save about $3,000 to be able to do the same thing.'

You see, Hank was trying to think about **how** he'd do it and because he couldn't imagine how, he'd never set climbing Uluru as a goal.

I told him to first write it as a goal and let his RAS do the rest. He was skeptical but said he'd give it a try and inform me of any progress. Over the next 6 months he reported that everywhere he looked, he saw stories about Uluru. He'd seen news articles, TV specials about Alice Springs, he'd noticed discount plane flights to Central Australia in his SPAM folder, he'd heard about a photographic exhibition that was coming to Central Australia and he'd rented the movie A Town Like Alice, which was filmed near Uluru. He had also talked to his friends about climbing Uluru and some had started sending him information on it. This information had always been around him but it was only brought to his attention by his RAS after he wrote it on his list.

Eight months after Hank had written down this goal, one of his friends called to tell him he had read that the Government was advertising for tradespeople to work on a gas pipeline near Alice Springs and they wanted qualified electricians! Hank couldn't believe it. He applied immediately — and got the job. He was contracted to work as an electrician in Alice Springs for 3 months. Hank was overwhelmed at how events had unfolded. After his first month in Alice Springs, Hank climbed

*Uluru – and was being paid to be there! You see, Hank had previously been thinking about how he might achieve the Uluru climb based on how I had done it with my conference. All he needed was to first decide that he **wanted** to do it, and let his RAS find the answers.*

Some of Hank's doubting friends said that it was probably just luck that Hank's friend spotted the advertisement. It wasn't luck. By first deciding to do it, Hank set the forces of his RAS in motion and that lead to the result. And none of his doubting friends has ever climbed the Rock – they probably can't imagine how they'd do it.

He later admitted that he had thought about the idea when he was younger but didn't know how he'd do it so never set it as a goal.

First decide *what* you want to do, not *how* you'll do it. The answers will begin to appear as soon as you've set the goal.

Clearly defined goals and life expectancy

Patrick Hill and Nicholas Turiano, of the Carleton University in Canada, analyzed data from over 6,000 participants who were a part of the *Midlife in the United States* study (MIDUS). They followed the subjects for an average of 14 years. They focused on participants' goals in life and their 'sense of purpose'. During the follow-up period, 569 of the participants had died. Hill and Turiano found that those who died had reported having fewer goals – if any – and a lower purpose in life than those who had survived. Overall, individuals who reported having goals and a greater purpose in life had a significantly lower mortality risk. The researchers also found that this association was true across all age groups.

**Research shows that setting clearly
defined goals increases your life
expectancy and leads to better health.**

Hill and Turiano's findings show that having a direction for your life and setting clear goals for what you want to achieve helps you live longer, regardless of when you find your purpose. So the earlier you start the process of setting clearly defined goals in your life, the earlier these protective effects will happen.

What people say on their deathbeds

In the final analysis, what do you think is really most important to most people? Australian palliative care nurse Bronnie Ware spent her days with people who had less than 12 weeks to live and who had been sent home to die. In her book, *The Top Five Regrets of the Dying*, Ware recorded what the dying had discussed about their lives. When asked about any regrets they had or anything they would do differently, common themes surfaced again and again.

Ware writes that people's five most common regrets when they are dying are: wishing they had been happier, had stayed in touch with their friends, had expressed their feelings, hadn't worked so hard, and had led the life they wanted to lead and not what was expected of them.

From the moment you lose your health, it's too late. Health brings a freedom very few people realise they possess until they no longer have it.

By simplifying your lifestyle and making conscious choices

along the way, it is possible to not need as much income as you perhaps think you do. And by creating more space in your life, you become happier and more open to new opportunities that are more suited to your new lifestyle.

Twists, turns and traps along the way...

Most people think that achieving a goal is a straightforward process maybe with a few bumps along the way. The reality is that the trip has twists, turns, traps, unexpected encounters and doors that will open that you could not see before. Sometimes you'll take a path toward a goal that you think you really want and, along the way, you might discover that you didn't really want it that much after all. But often you won't know what you really want until you get started on it. At other times you may experience things that, at the time of writing down the goal, may have seemed minor to you but can evolve into a major life experience, just like Barbara and my Russian experience.

You often don't know how you'll feel about any goal experience until you get into it. That's why you need a longer list of real and possible goals. I thought I'd love tap-dancing but it wasn't what I expected, so I replaced this goal with a new one – learning English jive – which Barb and I both love. Barbara thought she'd be a natural at piano playing and speaking German but it turned out she didn't enjoy either. On our eventual deathbeds, Barbara and I won't wonder what it would have been like to have lived in France, to have given seminars in Russia, sailed a super-yacht, tap-danced, scuba dived or owned a beautiful home full of kids. We wrote these dreams on paper, gave them deadlines and they came true.

Have at least ten possible goals on your list at any one

time. Most people – if they even have a goal – have only one goal. If that goal doesn't work out, they become despondent. Or they stick with a goal that they don't even enjoy any more. With a list of at least ten goals, if one no longer suits you, you have nine more and so you'll remain positive.

As we are writing this chapter, I am learning to play the saxophone and how to record, mix and master music in our new recording studio. I am also learning to drive a Bobcat and to speak Russian. Barbara is learning to be an excellent swimmer, is teaching reading classes at a primary school, is learning to be a good tennis player and is halfway towards her black belt in martial arts.

So what will you achieve this year and how will your life be more enriched? How will you be a better person, and a more interesting person a year from now?

There are two types of people – those who have 10 years of experience and those who have one year of experience repeated ten times over. The first type achieves more things in life, lives longer and has more fun.

Summary

- Set clearly defined goals, handwrite them in a list and keep adding to it.
- Goals give you a longer, healthier, happier life and let you reach your true potential.
- Be sure that what you set as goals are the things you really want and not what others expect of you.
- Write and rewrite your lists. Have they changed?
- Start writing a list of goals.

And start now.

**'It's better to look back on life and say,
"I can't believe I did that," than to look back
and say, "I wish I had done that."
Lucille Ball**

Chapter 4

Make a Plan with a Deadline

THE DOER

THE THINKER

**When you put a deadline on your dreams,
they become goals.**

When you decide to create a plan of action for your life and you begin to analyse where you stand now and where you are going, generalisations will no longer suit you. Have you ever noticed how much work you get done on the day before you leave for a holiday?

It's because you have a deadline looming and there are tasks that you need to finish before you go. Deadlines will spur you on, pushing you to complete the current projects.

**A deadline is to your goals
what the trigger is on a gun.**

Having a deadline will force you to move forward. You will need to work hard to reach your goal by the deadline, and as the deadline draws nearer it will inspire you to focus in order to achieve results. A deadline drives you toward consistent progress on your goals without the need for huge doses of willpower or outstanding motivation. Your RAS takes over.

If you pick up a 1-kilo weight, your mind prepares your body and your muscles to lift that much weight. If you decide to lift a 40-kilo weight, your mind also adjusts your body to lift that much weight. But if you thought that the 40-kilo weight only weighed 1 kilo, you could hurt your body trying to pick it up because your brain had only prepared it to lift 1 kilo. And so it is when you set a deadline. Your mind prepares your body for the task ahead by giving it more strength, more energy and a greater sense of urgency.

The word 'deadline' was first used in 1864 at Andersonville prison in the USA: 'On the inside of the stockade and 20 feet from it there is a dead-line established, over which no prisoner is allowed to go, day or night, under penalty of being shot.'

You can see this effect in any sport that has a deadline on it. As time runs out, the players move faster, try harder and seem to have more energy. A deadline keeps you focused on the result of your goal so you become more resistant to obstacles and to negative comments from others.

A written deadline instructs your body chemistry to move forward and begin to take action with a greater sense of urgency.

For the reasons previously mentioned, your deadline must also be in writing because your RAS will involve you more emotionally in your plans and will help you fight off fear, worry, doubt and procrastination.

Once you have decided what goal you will achieve, collect every piece of information you see, read or hear about it. Remember that as soon as you set the goal, the answers will begin to appear all around you. When you feel you have as much detail as you need to know about it and you can see how it can work, you then prioritise it as an **A** or **B** on your list and give it a deadline for its achievement.

Three ways to make a deadline work

1. *Make it realistic* – Set a time limit that can actually be achieved.
2. *Make it push you* – The shorter the deadline, the better the outcome.
3. *Take action now* – Don't keep thinking it over. Just start. Make adjustments as they are needed but don't wait; the time will never be exactly right.

**You don't have to be great to get started.
But you have to get started to become great.**

Break it down into small bites
As an old saying goes, *'How do you eat an elephant?
One bite at a time!'* Break your goals down into manageable
pieces; this makes them less daunting. If you spend too much
time contemplating the distance between where you stand
now and where you want to get to, there's a high risk that
you'll never start. Break your larger goals down into annual,
monthly, weekly, daily and even hourly ones. Breaking up
projects into a series of smaller tasks makes them easier to
complete and prevents you from waiting until the last minute
to finish your work.

By creating a series of realistic mini-goals along the way,
you can also feel a constant and building sense of achievement,
spurring you on to work even harder. Work backward from
your end goal. Each time you identify a smaller goal, see if
that can be broken down into more mini-goals. By logically
working back from everything you need to do to achieve
your goal, you can create tasks and a timeframe.

Keep your eyes on the next step, not the summit
In 1981, researchers Albert Bandura and Dale Schunk
conducted a test with children aged seven to ten. About half
the children were asked to set a goal of completing six pages
of maths problems per session. The researchers suggested to
the other half that they set a goal of completing 42 pages of

maths problems over seven sessions. The children with the smaller sub-goals had faster completion rates and more accurate answers than those with one large goal.

There is real power in the creation of small, manageable steps. This way you keep your mind confidently on what you know you can achieve, and you don't feel intimidated by the size of your goal.

A TRUE STORY – BARBARA AND ALLAN PEASE

When Barbara began selling advertising in 1981 her goal was to achieve over $1 million in sales that year. In 1971, Allan had the same goal – to sell over $1 million in life insurance in a year. They both wrote down their clearly defined goals and each set a deadline of 12 months in which to achieve it. A million dollars in any business was a huge goal back then and a daunting one to tackle. When they broke their goals down into manageable bites, though, it started to look possible. A million dollars in a year works out at $20,000 a week over 50 weeks; this means $4,000 a day in sales if you work five days a week. For Barbara, this meant four sales a week at an average of $5,000 per sale, and the numbers were similar for Allan.

Assuming they could each sell to one in three of their presentations, this meant making 12 solid presentations a week. If one out of every three prospects agreed to an interview, it meant contacting seven prospects every day to ask for an appointment; this could be achieved in less than an hour a day. While an annual goal of $1 million of anything can seem daunting, calling seven prospects in an hour each day is very achievable.

Take action now

As soon as you've decided what you are going to do – get started. Not tomorrow, next week, after Christmas, when the kids leave home or when Halley's Comet flies over to give you the starting signal. **Start right now**. Enrol in that course, apply for that interview, join the club that teaches you how to do what you want to achieve, find a mentor, or sign up as an apprentice. Pick up the phone and call someone who can tell you where to begin. The most important action to take is to get moving.

The reason most people don't do more with their lives is because they are always busy getting ready to get ready. Yesterday, you probably said 'tomorrow'. The right time will never come. Start now. Because now is all you have. Twenty years from now you will be more disappointed by the things you didn't do than by the things you did do. You don't have to see the whole staircase – **just take the first step.**

Sometimes the smallest step in the right direction can be the biggest step of your life. Even if you have to tiptoe, take that step.

When you take action on your plans, your RAS triggers the effect that is known as the Law of Attraction. The things you want suddenly seem to become attracted to you, and like-minded people appear around you. Others begin volunteering information that can help you move forward, and people with similar goals become your allies. Where you previously saw some things as difficult to tackle, you begin to see ways to handle them. Things that were once vague become clearer and the answers you need start to materialise all around you.

As soon as you've decided what your goal will be, start working on it immediately to reach it.

While having a plan is a critical part of success, many people become so involved in planning that they don't get started. Step onto the playing field immediately, experience what it's like being out there, and start learning what to do. Don't let your plan be an excuse for a slow start. Get moving while you are hot to trot. Don't wait till you pay off your mortgage, the kids leave home, till you gain more confidence, till after the New Year or your birthday or the next Blue Moon, or until you are married, divorced, separated, promoted, retired, made redundant or your parrot dies. Start now!

If 'Plan A' doesn't work there are another 25 letters in the alphabet.

What if you can't make a deadline?

Sometimes, the result can take longer to achieve than you originally thought. If this happens, break down the goal into smaller goals, and set another deadline and then another if necessary. A deadline is an estimate of when you feel you can achieve your goal, but sometimes a few adjustments along the way might be necessary. The more practice you have at setting deadlines, the more accurate you will soon become at predicting timeframes.

A TRUE STORY – ALLAN PEASE

One day, when I was five years old, I was out of my depth in a swimming pool and almost drowned. That memory has remained with me ever since. When I was 14, I set a goal to earn the Surf Life-Saving Bronze Medallion and so I joined the life-saving club, but my father's job was relocated and our family moved to Melbourne.

*I never finished the Bronze Medallion training, but I left this goal on my list as a **B** item because I really wanted to achieve it.*

Twenty-five years later, at age 39, I joined the Avalon Life-Saving Club in Sydney, enrolled in the Bronze Medallion training course and started again. The course required being proficient in a variety of skills ranging from cardio resuscitation to surf rescue, and using a range of equipment including life vests, boards and surf boats. It also demanded various physical fitness tests, including running and swimming. The physical training was intensive, especially for a man approaching 40. The other participants on the course were aged between 17 and 22, and the pressure was on me to keep up with them. After a decade of martial arts training I was fit enough to handle it all – until the swimming test. This involved swimming half a kilometre in under eight minutes. From a fitness viewpoint this was not a problem for me, but it meant I needed a strong, effective swimming style and this required me to keep my face down in the water. To my horror I found that, at age 39, I was still the prisoner of my near-drowning at age 5.

Even though I'd been surfing for years, I simply couldn't keep my face down in the water to swim fast enough to make the necessary time to pass the test. The easy answer here could have been to quit, but I really wanted to do this so I enrolled in a swimming class.

Picture this scene: I'm sitting on the edge of the swimming pool with six other classmates, aged between four and six. I'm clutching a small plastic kickboard and receiving instructions from the teacher. I am having a serious issue with my face-in-the-water problem and the kids' mothers are having a secret laugh about this older guy who obviously can't swim properly.

The teacher broke us up into pairs. My teammate, six-year-old Danny, was feeling sorry for me in my moments of struggle as I continually failed to keep my face in the water while swimming up and down the pool with my little kickboard.

'You can use my board if you want to,' he whispered sympathetically. 'It goes faster than yours.'

'They all go the same speed!' I snapped, feeling anxious and inept. But as I looked at the tiny, startled face of this well-meaning six-year-old motivational consultant, I agreed to swap boards with him. I decided that if Danny could do it, I would too.

After six classes and lots of practice, I passed the face-in-the-water test in my swimming class and, a week later, my surf swimming trials (three seconds under time) and was awarded the Surf Bronze Medallion.

If achieving your goal means you have to learn to swim with four-year-olds, then that's what you do, regardless of your age.

How far are you prepared to go to reach your goals? When your goals are clearly defined and you have a plan with a deadline, you are far less likely to quit, whatever the circumstances. I had waited 25 years to reset the deadline on this goal and I wasn't going to quit and start again. The only obstacle in my way was the face-in-the-water problem. I had set the goal to earn the Bronze Medallion at age 14 and finally achieved it when I was almost 40. It had taken another 25 years for my life circumstances to be right to allow me to tackle it again as an **A** goal.

The important thing is that I had decided **what** I wanted to do and only set the deadline when the time was right. When you define a goal, you don't have to start on it immediately unless it is a number-one priority. You can't start all goals at the same time. Set your deadline to begin when you feel the time is right. I set this deadline twice. You don't have to give up on a goal just because circumstances change. Circumstances are often temporary. But remember, until you set a deadline nothing will happen. A deadline galvanises you into action.

A year from now you'll wish you'd started today. And if not now, when?

A TRUE STORY – ALLAN AND BARBARA

When Barbara and I discovered that our accountant had been lying to us about our investments, we were shocked. But it was too late – everything we owned was gone and we had to sell our remaining assets to pay the last debts of over $2,000,000. Twenty years of the Body Language project – the books, films, training films and success – had suddenly gone. We struggled financially over the next two years to pay the debts and I became depressed, blaming myself for what had happened.

After two years of my negative thinking, self-criticism, colds, flus, lethargy, sleep disorders and thyroid tumours, Barbara had had enough. 'Put a deadline on it, Allan!' she barked at me one morning. What? A deadline on feeling depressed?

Like many men, I was in denial about my depression. I knew that we all have a choice about what thoughts we put into our minds and we can choose 100 per cent of those thoughts, but I had never considered that this could be an option for being depressed. So if negative thinking about our circumstances had made me become continually ill and not a fun person to be around, it made sense that I could put a deadline on being depressed and only think positive thoughts after that deadline.

Putting a deadline on negative thinking

Negative thinking becomes a life habit and a comfortable way of behaving for some people. Unless someone points it out to you, you can easily become a habitual negative thinker. The best the doctors could offer me was Prozac. Instead, I decided to put a deadline on my negative thinking.

From that deadline date I resolved only to think about what I did want to happen, and not what I didn't want.

One of the first signs of depression is losing your sense of humour and not seeing the funny side of things.

It was a Tuesday morning when I chose the deadline of 4 p.m. on the Friday of the following week. Until that Friday, I could be a real negative ass if I so chose. Importantly, that would give me time to grow used to the idea of only thinking about what I did want, instead of what I didn't want, which is what I'd been doing for over two years. At 4 p.m. on that Friday I said to Barbara, 'Okay...I'm back! From today, we'll only think about what we CAN do.' I remember that moment clearly. It was an incredibly liberating experience and I immediately felt a sense of calm and optimism, something that I hadn't felt in a long time. I was back in the driver's seat. And it was my 45th birthday.

'If you're going through hell, keep going.'
Winston Churchill

Barb and I then made the decision that we would never again be caught in these circumstances and that we would once more become successful. We had no idea how we would do it – we simply decided that we would do it. That was the most important thing. And my sense of humour quickly started to return.

If you find yourself depressed or down,
put a deadline on it.

Summary

If you're stressed, worried or depressed about any of the things in your life and your negative thoughts have become a habit, put a deadline on when you will get over them. Decide that, from a specific time on a specific day, you will not think negatively about the things that happened to you in the past. Decide to think only about what you *do* want. It's that simple. Not always easy to do, but that simple.

Every person who lives to an old age will have at least three major disasters happen to them in their life, such as divorce, illness, bankruptcy, redundancy, or the death of a loved one. Disasters happen to us all; they are a part of life. But just because you get knocked down doesn't mean you're out of the game. You are only defeated if you stay down. Decide in advance that when tragedy strikes, you'll pull yourself out of it.

- A dream is just a dream until you put a deadline on it.
- Deadlines demand action and will drive you forward.
- You can put a deadline on anything, including negative thinking.
- For big goals, break them down into bite-sized pieces and eat one piece at a time.
- If you don't think you will reach an important deadline, adjust it.
- Make your deadline realistic, make it short enough to push you.

And do it **now**. List at least five of your goals below with a deadline.

GOAL	DEADLINE

Life is like a camera. Focus on what's important. Capture the good times and develop from the negatives. And if things don't work out, just take another shot.

Chapter 5

Follow Through, Despite What Others Think, Do or Say

For many people, following through on their plans can be the hardest part in the goal-getting process. You've set a specific goal, written a plan with a deadline, and now you are announcing it to the world. But suddenly you find a flood of people – especially relatives and friends – trying to talk you out of it. They tell you you're too old, too young, too fat, too thin, it's too risky, it's bad timing, the economy is weak, you're too broke, you lack experience, there is inflation, deflation, you're not talented enough, you are too lazy or too crazy.

They ask, '*Why would you want to do that at this point in*

your life? You might get sick/killed/injured or cheated going to places/jobs/cities/careers or countries like that! You can't go now because you're married/divorced/single/broke/doing well/doing poorly or have too much debt, commitment or family. If you fail, who will look after your partner/wife/husband/kids/house/career/dog or sick grandmother?'

Decide right now that you will not listen to these people. We are not saying that you should be reckless or take unnecessary risks – every choice you make to move forward has risks. You need to make your own informed decisions – don't let anyone steal your dreams. People who are too weak to follow their own dreams will always find a way to discourage yours. Don't let small minds convince you that your goals are too big. If your goals don't scare you a little, they are not big enough.

Be careful who you open up to. Only tell your dreams to a few people who really care. The rest are just curious.

Why others try to talk you out of your goals

There are three main reasons why others – friends, and especially relatives – will try to dissuade you from attempting certain goals.

1. They are worried.
They are genuinely concerned for you and they don't want you to lose your money, health or opportunity, or for you to go backward in life. '*If you become an aid worker in Africa,*

there are animals, spiders, mosquitoes and terrorists that can kill you.'

2. You'll show them up.

When you attempt certain goals, you highlight how little others are doing with their own lives. You will understand this when you realise that the reasons others give you for not proceeding are *their* reasons, not yours. *'Going into a new business right now is dangerous because you have kids to feed, a mortgage to pay, the economy is weak and people are relying on you. You should wait until things improve.'*

3. They become intimidated.

Setting and attaining new and exciting goals can make others feel threatened or inadequate about their own lives or their personal lack of achievements. *'Climb Mount Kilimanjaro? What would that prove? Here, have another doughnut.'*

People will often attempt to divert you from your goals because of their own genuine, selfish or manipulative reasons. This is why the last step of this process is to follow through with your plan, despite what others may say, do or think. Thank them for their concerns and interest, tell them you love them (where necessary), but restate what you intend to do and why you will do it. If they persist in diverting you, sincerely thank them again and restate your goal without explanation. Then, just do it. The only people who can offer you real insights into what you want to achieve are those who have either done it or are currently doing it. Otherwise, they can only give an opinion based on what they would do in their circumstances. Never make decisions on the advice of others who don't have to live with the results.

**When you are writing the story of your life,
don't let anyone else hold the pen.**

The fear of failure

Many people don't start on the path to reaching their goals because they are afraid of failure. Failure is an important part of success and few people have ever succeeded at anything without first failing several times. **Winners are not people who never fail. Winners are people who never quit.** If you give up too soon you'll never know what you missed. Any mistake you make simply helps you to learn the right way to make something work. A boxer doesn't lose the match because he gets knocked down, he only loses if he doesn't get back up.

**'The master has failed more times than
the beginner has even tried.'
Zig Ziglar, American Author and
Motivational Speaker**

If J. K. Rowling had been discouraged by the first ten publishers who knocked her back, Harry Potter would never have existed. If Howard Schultz had given up after 242 rejections by banks and lenders, there would be no Starbucks. If Walt Disney had quit after his theme park idea suffered over 300 rejections, there would be no Disneyland.

**'Rock bottom became the solid foundation
on which I rebuilt my life.'
J. K. Rowling**

How to avoid being manipulated by others

Here is a simple but powerful technique for dealing with people who attempt to stop you reaching your goals, or who just want to control you. With this technique, you either agree with them, or you agree with their right to an opinion – however uninformed, unfounded or manipulative their opinion may seem to you.

Technique number 1: Agree with the truth

The most powerful response you can give your critic is to agree with the truth of what they say and then to restate your position.

Example 1
Mother: *If you go to work in Africa, you could die from a deadly disease.*
Daughter: *You could be right. But I feel compelled to help the underprivileged – and I can't wait to go.*

The daughter has *agreed with the truth* of her mother's criticism, while at the same time maintaining her own position.

Example 2
Sue: *I don't think you should quit your job, Brandon. You're a key person in that company and if the economy goes bad you'll still have a job. Going into business alone has no guarantees.*
Brandon: *You're absolutely right, Sue. There are no guarantees – but I know I'll do well and I'm really looking forward to this opportunity.*
Brandon agreed with the truth of what Sue said. He didn't argue with her or put himself or her down. At the same time, he maintained his position without being aggressive. Where you might have normally told someone to drop dead, mind their own business or blow it out their ass, you have agreed with them, restated your position and no-one feels wrong or threatened.

Technique number 2: Agree with your critic's right to an opinion

Often, you will disagree with your critic's opinion, but you can still agree with their right to have one, however silly you think it may be.

Example 1
Dave: *If you sell your home to buy two smaller units, you won't be living as comfortably as you are now.*
Monica: *I understand why you might feel that way, Dave, but I want to be a millionaire by the time I'm thirty and this is a major step toward it.*

Example 2
Leanne: *Why would you want to buy a Mazda, Glen? You know Toyotas are much better cars.*

Glen: *I understand your opinion, Leanne, and you're right – Toyotas are great cars – but I just love the feel of the Mazda.*

Glen and Monica both agreed with their critic's right to an opinion – Glen also agreed with the truth – but neither backed away from their position or made the other person feel wrong. Even when you completely disagree with someone's criticism of you, there is usually a way to be agreeable while affirming what you will continue to do. Your aim should be to always make others feel right, even when you don't agree with them.

If anyone ever tells you your dreams are stupid, remember that there's a multi-millionaire somewhere who invented the Pool Noodle.

Summary

The difference between successful people and the rest is that successful people are action-oriented. They might not look very graceful when they begin, but they are moving forward. And they stay on track despite other people's attempts to dislodge them.

Well-meaning friends, relatives or others may try to stop you from moving toward your goals because they either love you, hate you, or don't want to look bad themselves. Never worry about people who talk behind your back – it means you must be two steps in front of them. If people are trying to bring you down it means you are above them. The only way to avoid criticism is to do nothing, say nothing and be nothing. When you set your goal and create a plan with a deadline, take that first step and move forward – despite what others may think, say or do.

You can only be shot in the ass when you are further up the ladder than the rest.

Be agreeable with everyone. Develop an agreeable nature and make others feel right, whatever their opinion. Agree with the truth. Let others know that you agree with something they said. Nod and say, 'Yes, you're right' or 'I agree with you.' At worst, agree with your critic's right to an opinion, even when you think they are talking complete nonsense. Acknowledge that it's all right for them to think that way while, at the same time, restating what you believe to be true.

Avoid arguing. You can rarely win an argument, even if you're right. Arguing loses friends and credibility and gives fighters what they want – a fight.

Never fight with pigs – you'll only get covered in mud.

Chapter 6

Take Responsibility for Your Life

How karma works

Before the Global Financial Crisis began in 2008, the Western world had experienced nearly 20 years of the richest times ever known. It became the norm in many countries for people to own a home, drive new cars, take overseas holidays, wear the latest fashions and drink lattes. It had become popular in Western countries to think that everyone was entitled to a rich, wealthy and fulfilling life, whether they had worked for it or not. While the Baby Boomers knew this concept was flawed, Generation X embraced the idea. For Generation Y, it was the only reality they knew.

This period created the kind of thinking that led many people to silently believe that someone, other than themselves, was responsible for delivering them a golden life – be it the government, their parents, society, corporations, unions, their bosses or the universe. They also believed that someone or something, other than themselves, was to blame for the negative aspects of their lives. People began blaming their circumstances on their spouse, their partner, their birthplace, other countries, the weather, their genes, the banks, refugees, religion, numerology, astrology, even the magnetic pull of the Moon.

But if you want to see who the actual person is behind your own circumstances, your current financial condition, your career, your health, and your relationship successes or failures, you just need to stand in front of a mirror.

It's you. You are responsible for the circumstances in your life right now, whether they are good or bad. Unless you have a medical reason such as schizophrenia or autism or have suffered irreparable brain damage, a debilitating medical condition or live in a totally repressed society, you are not just partly responsible for where you are now, you are completely responsible. The way you think and the choices you made in the past have created the circumstances you find yourself in now.

If your life is an outstanding success, you are responsible for that result. If it isn't, you are also responsible. So take all the credit, good or bad.

To be fair, your parents, society, culture, religion and upbringing fed into your RAS what you now believe. It is those beliefs that have brought you to where you are today. But now that you understand how your RAS works, you are completely responsible for your life from now on. Accept that you are the one who has directly or indirectly created the world you live in. It was you who accepted the job you currently work in and you who decided to stay in it, even if you realised it wasn't your passion.

It was you who decided to regularly eat junk food and it was your arm that pushed the junk food into your mouth. You were the one who chose not to exercise regularly; and it was you who chose brainless logic to defend self-destructive habits like smoking, drinking, speeding, using drugs or having abusive partners. It was you who didn't say 'No' to the person or people who asked you to do things you didn't want to do, and it was you who decided to trust the person who let you down. It was you who refused to put boundaries on your children, your relatives or the people who cause you the most grief in your life. It was you who chose to stay in a relationship that was abusive or didn't have a future.

If you have employees or customers who drive you insane, or any friends who are selfish, all-about-me jerks, you have chosen to have them in your life. If the people around you make you unhappy it's not their fault – it's yours. They are in your personal or professional life because you drew them to you, and you let them stay. You made the choices, you thought the thoughts and you have created the circumstances you are now in. And it is you who is making the excuses to yourself and to others about why you are where you are in life right now.

If you are feeling any sort of anger or offence about what you have just read, then reread it because you definitely need to hear it again. Outside environments may have fed your RAS in the past, but you are consciously in charge of what goes into it from now on.

Taking immediate responsibility for your own circumstances in life means that whatever happens from today on, you will approach every event objectively. From now on, you will ask yourself, 'What did I do to get this outcome?'; 'What was I thinking to attract these circumstances?'; 'What did I say or not say to make that person respond the way they did?'; 'What did I believe that contributed to this result?'; 'What can I do now to get a different outcome?'

Take control of your life now

The great news is that taking full and immediate responsibility for your circumstances puts you in the driver's seat of your own life. It puts you in charge of where you can go. It means you will begin to analyse the outcome of every event that happens in your life. You will start to use your RAS to get better outcomes for yourself. While you may not have control over some of the things that happen in life, you do have complete control over what thoughts you think, how you react, and the choices you make about what happens. And those thoughts, reactions and choices are what will create your next set of circumstances. It's you who are in charge of these things – and you always have been, whether you realised it or not.

'The only thing we have control over is our thoughts and attitudes. If you make a bad decision, it's how you deal with it that is important, and that means you bring it back into your control.'
Rita Hartney, author of
It's Time for Women to Take Control

Your choices

Everything you have in life is based on the choices you make. The choices you made in the past are the reasons for the situation you are in now, be it a positive or negative one. And now it is you and you alone who are responsible for every decision you make in your life and every direction you choose to take. To think otherwise is to refuse to take responsibility for your life. Every person born today has the opportunity to take charge of his or her own life and to be responsible for every outcome. But, you may ask, what about people who are born into poverty, or are in countries where there are forced marriages, or where the law works against your potential success or you may be killed for having your own opinion?

A TRUE STORY – STEVEN

I was born in a country where the government and society decided what I would think or do. My sister was forced into an arranged marriage and many of my friends were jailed, beaten or killed because of their opinions. But I realised that I still had a choice – to stay or to leave. My choice was to leave my country and to have the chance to choose my own future as a refugee.

I walked over 3,000 kilometres and I now live elsewhere. I have a new name, a new life and a good job, despite having only one hand. Many of my friends chose to stay in my old country and they are still victims of that choice. My choice was to take a risk and to start again and I now receive the rewards of that choice. I did not end up where I originally thought I would, but as I headed toward a life in a new country, doors opened for me that I could not have seen if I had never chosen to leave.

Of course, the risk was always there that I might have been captured and killed, but it was still a choice to stay or to escape.

If you want to receive the benefits of life, you must take the necessary risks. It does not matter what your circumstances are now or how you got there — you still have the power to choose new circumstances for yourself. Do not be a victim by blaming your environment or your circumstances. You always have the power to choose the way something will end.

Events you can't control

Life is full of events over which we have little or no control. For example, a tsunami or bushfire can wipe out your home, a drunk driver can involve you in an accident, or you can contract a life-threatening illness. But what you need to do is have 100 per cent control over your thoughts, actions and responses to what happens to you. Those thoughts, actions and responses are the choices that will affect what your future will be. Your life is the result of the choices you make.

Your life is a result of the choices you make. If you don't like your life, start making better choices.

A TRUE STORY – W. MITCHELL

At age 27, Mitchell was in a blazing motorcycle accident that burned 65 per cent of his body. Four years later, when he had recovered, Mitchell decided to gain a pilot's licence but a plane he was in crashed and he was sentenced to life in a wheelchair. Throughout his recovery process, Mitchell was determined to prosper, to maintain control and to deal with the countless changes to his life — whatever the outcome. Through strength and determination, he allowed change to become a positive force in facing the impossible.

'It's not what happens to you, it's what you do about it' became his mantra. His seemingly hopeless story evolved into an amazing life of achievement that has inspired millions around the world.

Following his accidents, Mitchell became an internationally acclaimed mayor who 'saved a mountain', a successful businessman who helped create jobs for thousands of people, a congressional nominee from Colorado, and a respected environmentalist and conservationist who repeatedly testified before Congress. He even continued his love of piloting airplanes and white-water rafting. Mitchell's astonishing accomplishments have received recognition in the media internationally. He is a bestselling author and was the subject of the television series, Super Humans. His life clearly illustrates his own philosophy that most limitations are self-imposed.

**'Before I was paralysed there were 10,000 things
I could do. Now there are 9,000.
I can either dwell on the 1,000 I've lost
or focus on the 9,000 I have left.'
W. Mitchell**

Stop making excuses

If you want to create a life that has everything in it that you could ever want, then you must stop making excuses for yourself. This means no more victim stories about someone who did you wrong, or about the external forces, events or people that you claim are preventing you from moving toward your dreams. In over 40 years of teaching others how to get what they want in life, we've heard every excuse for why someone can't move forward right now. It's the fault of the government, their gender, their ex-partner, the economy, their skin colour, their boss, in-laws, their current partner, their health, and so on. We've heard golfers blaming the course, their clubs, the weather or their partners for why they played badly. While some of these factors may be true, they don't decide the overall outcome of golf. Tiger Woods, Jack Nicklaus and Ernie Els never would have succeeded if their clubs, the courses or the weather were the controlling factors in golf. If Bill Gates, Mark Zuckerberg, Mother Teresa or Steve Jobs had decided that government policy, the weather, the bank or their birthplace were limiting factors there would never have been Microsoft, Facebook, the Missionaries of Charity or Apple. For every so-called 'limiting factor' that exists in every pursuit, there are thousands of people who have succeeded in that pursuit despite those 'limiting factors'.

If 'limiting factors' were really important no-one would ever achieve anything.

The truth is that you chose the thoughts that have put you where you are right now. You always have. But it doesn't even matter why you made the choices you made in the past – that's the past. Your future will be determined by the thoughts and choices you make from today – and you have 100 per cent control over those thoughts and choices.

The only difference is that now you can begin choosing the life circumstances you really want. Your RAS won't fail you. That's why what you are reading here is so powerful. Decide right now to stop making excuses for things in your life.

**There are only two options – make progress
or make excuses.**

When you make a poor choice

Making a bad choice doesn't mean you're stupid. The consequences of a poor choice are life's way of telling you you needed to learn a lesson. If you make the same poor choice a second time, then life will show you again that you still haven't learned your lesson. If you continue to make the same mistake repeatedly, then you probably have an issue such as self-sabotaging and need advice from a professional coach or counsellor. Nothing ever goes away until it teaches you what you need to know.

**When you continually repeat a mistake
it's not a mistake any more – it's a choice.**

Why you've got what you've got

Most people have the bizarre idea that you can keep repeating the same behaviours over and over while somehow expecting to achieve a different result. The reason you have the life you have now and the things you own now is because you keep repeating the same ways of thinking and behaving. If you want different results – the kind of results that will dramatically change and improve your life and lead you to your dreams – then you must start thinking and behaving differently from the way you have been so far. If you continue to think and act as you have until now, you'll continue to achieve just more of the same results you've been getting.

That's why you are where you are in life right now, and why you've got what you've got. You are repeating the same thought processes and decisions.

If you continue to do what you've always done, you'll get more of what you've got.

The results you have been getting in your life so far are the consequences of your choices, thoughts and behaviour. And results don't lie. You are fat, thin or average weight – or you're not. You're either rich or you're not. Your family either respects you or they don't. You either have the things you want in life or you don't. Results don't lie.

Your results tell you the truth.

From today, stop kidding yourself that you are a victim of circumstances. Stop telling others that things are not your fault. They *are* your fault. They are your doing from your thinking, and it is your responsibility to change or to not change. Your results are telling you the truth about your choices. Your RAS needs to be reprogrammed.

Quit complaining

By definition, by complaining you are saying that you want something better than what you have – a better house, car, partner, health, job and so on. But complaining also tells the listener that you are not prepared to take the actions or risks necessary to achieve those results. Whining is making the same complaint over and over with absolutely no intention of taking affirmative action.

Even when someone feels they have a legitimate complaint about something – such as the amount of work they've been given, poor treatment by their partner, or bad customer service they've received – they usually complain to the wrong person. They complain to their friends that their husband/wife/partner treats them badly; they complain to their partner that their boss is too demanding; or they complain to their neighbour that the local store gave them bad service. These complaints are pointless because the person they are complaining to can't do anything about the complaint and possibly doesn't even care.

Don't complain. As the old joke goes, 'Eighty per cent of people don't care about your problems – and the rest are glad.'

On the flip side, most people compliment the wrong people. They tell the waiter in a restaurant how wonderful the food was or how much they enjoyed it. But the waiter doesn't care: often he just wants you to give a good tip and go home. If you feel you have a real complaint – or compliment – about the food, tell the cook, not the waiter. Better still, if you don't like the food, take affirmative action and choose a nicer restaurant next time. It's preferable to try a new restaurant than to attempt to retrain the chef in a bad one by complaining.

When you complain about your life you focus on the things you don't want, and so your RAS looks for more circumstances similar to the ones that got you to where you are now. Complaining reinforces negative neural pathways in your brain and your RAS creates repetition of the negative things you already have in your life.

If you want the things in your life to change, change the things in your life.

Take affirmative action toward your goals and focus only on the things you do want. And stop complaining – now. If you have a legitimate complaint about anything, tell the right person – someone who can do something about it.

Choose your own circumstances

Earl Nightingale was a pioneer of self-development skills and one of my mentors in the 1970s. He taught me that I could choose my own circumstances by making positive choices about what I wanted and, if I didn't, the circumstances I didn't want would choose me. While this idea can sound unsettling to some people, it's liberating because it means that you can go anywhere you choose in life instead of being dragged along in a current by everyone else's circumstances, or by their opinions of you.

**People who don't take 100 per cent
personal responsibility for their lives end
up working for those who do.**

As we mentioned several times – you are responsible for where you are in life right now. We are not talking here about someone with AIDS born into poverty in Ethiopia – we are talking about you. Your past thoughts and actions have brought you to where you are today. When you faced events you couldn't control, your responses to those events contributed to your current circumstances.

The consequences of negative thoughts

Let's say you secretly complain to your co-workers that your boss is a dimwit who couldn't make an intelligent decision to save his life. Your boss hears about your comment and fires you. It's easy to see how your actions brought about your current circumstances – that is, you're now unemployed. But what about the fact that you were too busy to take that extra-curricular study or self-development course and then you saw your company promote someone below you who had less experience?

Perhaps in your personal life you chose a partner, or keep choosing partners, who mentally or physically abuse you and you decide to stay with them, using the usual clichés *'Because I love him/her'*; *'I do it for the sake of the kids'*; *'We have history/finances together'*, and other excuses that mask your lack of affirmative action?

Or you say you were too busy, too tired or distracted to give time to your children, who are now a social embarrassment to you?

Or you pretend that you're somehow not responsible for your size or weight?

Every time you point your finger forward there are at least three fingers pointing back at you.

When it comes to your health, do you claim you are the victim of hormones, bad genes, your upbringing or that you've given birth to three kids? Or that you are a victim of the random fat globules that float around in space and only stick to certain people?

No! You chose not to learn about or take action on diet and exercise – and so you are ultimately responsible. Do you prefer to act bewildered about your weight or even blame your arm for continually putting junk food into your mouth? No. Your arm doesn't work independently – you instructed it to shove the junk into your mouth. You did it, and you did it when no-one was looking. That way you could claim with a confused look, 'I don't know why I put on weight – I don't eat that much...'

Whichever way you want to look at it, your actions – or lack of action – directly contributed to the circumstances you are in right now. As we have said, you did it – not 'them', those faceless people who dictate our choices. It was you.

If you don't like something, change it. If you can't change it, change the way you think about it.

Taking responsibility for your health

Over 80 per cent of cancers and heart disease are life-style-related – poor diet, smoking, alcohol, eating junk food, pollution, stressful living and negative attitudes. From 2015, more than 50 per cent of the populations of nations that eat Western diets and live Western lifestyles will get cancer of some type. Barbara and I constantly see self-delusion about who or what is responsible for cancer when we meet people who have a cancer diagnosis. We counsel people with and without cancer on how to change their lifestyle to one that carries lower cancer risks – such as eating organic food, becoming vegetarian, quitting smoking and drinking, taking regular exercise, limiting stress, thinking positive thoughts, and so on.

While most cancer patients see the wisdom of doing these things, few actually continue to keep these changes in their lives after their cancer treatment. The majority go back to living and thinking in the ways they did prior to their cancer diagnosis. Most of them repeat the lifestyle and behaviours that contributed to their cancer in the first place. They don't change. They delegate the responsibility of their health to their doctor, a health expert, radiologist, spouse or God. They refuse to take responsibility for their own circumstances. And we regularly see these people die, largely because they won't acknowledge that they are responsible for their own health.

Take responsibility for staying current

Do not ignore the warning signs of potential problems or of major life changes. Choosing inaction instead of action is one of the main reasons why so many people achieve so little with their lives.

Think of an older person you know who proudly declares that they do not have an email address or Internet access. They are completely unaware that they have not only relegated themselves to the bottom of most career opportunities; they now have little, if any, ability to converse with younger people about the world. Older people who act in this way are oblivious to the fact that they have completely sidelined themselves from the realities of 21st-century life. Ignoring changing trends is a common theme in the lives of many people as they grow older.

I can recall people telling me in the 1970s that mobile phones (I had one of the first) would never catch on and that if they wanted to make a phone call, they'd stop at a phone box. I can still hear supposedly intelligent people saying that email was a waste of time, online dating would only ever be used by perverts and paedophiles, and that they would never use SMS or Facebook because they don't want to hear about what people had for breakfast. So they ignore the world as it changes and thereby limit their capability to move forward into new and exciting areas, and lose the ability to converse with their children and grandchildren.

Don't live in the past – take responsibility for staying current.

Take responsibility for who you let into your life

Listen to the subtle clues about people. Human resource managers understand that a person's track record and past performance is the best indicator of how they will perform in the future. If a person is often rude, late, arrogant, didn't pay their bills, was abusive, alcoholic, drug-addicted, obsessive, untidy, lazy, and so on, you can reasonably assume that these habits will recur in their future performance.

The way people treat you is a statement about who they are – it's not a statement about you.

Sure, a small percentage of people can alter their lives and do better, but it usually takes a life-changing event, such as a cancer diagnosis, a religious experience, the death of a loved one or a near-death experience to bring about any change. Most people rarely change much in their lives. Most people are not reading books like this one – books that can give you the answers to questions about how to be successful, that can teach you what you need to know or that hold a mirror up to your life.

Don't ignore life's warnings. The way a person treats waiters, hotel staff and dogs is the way they will eventually treat their husband, wife or partner. Life sends you clues about everyone and everything. If someone is detrimental to your life, get them out of it, sideline them or at least plan to spend less time around them.

A TRUE STORY – ANNE

Anne was raised in a family where her father was emotionally cold, alcoholic and physically abusive. Like most kids under seven years old, she had always tried to win his affection and get him to love her. As an adult she was continually attracted to men who mentally and physically abused her, and this became one of her life themes. She was unwittingly selecting partners who had her father's traits and was trying to get them to love her. Anne eventually married a man who also abused her and made her financially bankrupt. At age 46, she made her first major positive decision – she divorced him.

Anne says that this was the best positive decision of her life. But she claims that the decision left her financially broke. She says it was not her fault, it was his. The truth is that by not taking responsibility for her past choices – picking abusive men – Anne caused her own emotional damage and financial losses. Her positive decision to divorce him ended that period of pain for her.

Today she has a new relationship with another man who also abuses her. Life sent her clear warnings but she ignored them and repeated what she'd always done.

Summary

The world does not pay you based on what you know. It pays you based on what you do. University students often make the mistake of assuming that once they graduate, the world will pay them. It won't. Everything you do is based on the choices you make. It's not your parents, your past relationships, your job, the economy, the weather, an argument or your age that is to blame. You, and only you, are responsible for every decision and choice you make. Period. The great news is that you have 100 per cent control over your choices from now on. In *The Answer* we are showing you how to live a 'want to' life, not a 'have to' life.

From today, decide to take 100 per cent responsibility for everything in your life. If you catch yourself complaining about anything, stop immediately. Decide right now to make changes to the ways you respond to the events in your life. You will immediately begin to see different outcomes to the ones you've been getting, and the paths toward your dreams will begin to materialise. Start talking positively about what you can do and **will** do.

If you find yourself with a group of people who bitch and complain about everyone and everything – leave that group. Accept that you chose to be with this group and that you can choose to find another, more positive one. Give yourself permission to walk away from anything that gives you bad vibes. You don't need to explain it to anybody, just trust your inner voice. Acknowledge today that you have been responsible for attracting to your life the things and people that now surround you. Decide immediately that you will only have the people and things that you really want and deserve in your life.

List ten things you wish you could change about yourself or that you wish you were better at. Look at the list to realise the negative feelings you hold and feel them drift away.

1. _____
2. _____
3. _____
4. _____
5. _____
6. _____
7. _____
8. _____
9. _____
10. _____

The best day of your life is the one on which you decide that your life is your own – no excuses or apologies, no-one to lean on, to rely on or to blame. This is the day your life really begins.

Don't blame anyone in your life. Good people give you happiness and bad people give you experience. The worst people give you lessons and the best people give you memories.

Chapter 7

The Art of Visualisation

Man, woman and dog – and what they see.

As you know, the RAS is the mechanism that searches for and identifies resources and information that you would not normally have noticed and which otherwise might have remained as 'background noise'. The secret to visualisation is that your RAS acts completely on what it is told. It can't distinguish between reality and fantasy and so it causes you to physically respond to a task as if it were actually happening. You create a specific picture of your goal in your conscious mind and the RAS then passes this to your subconscious, which will consequently propel you toward your goal.

Visualisation means closing your eyes and vividly imagining the achievement of the goals you've set. You imagine what you would be doing, how it would feel, and you see yourself achieving the results you want. Studies have found that students who visualise in advance the results they want can, on average, achieve 100 per cent greater results than their peers who did not use visualisation.

How the mind works

Your mind cannot tell the difference between real or imagined events, so it doesn't know whether you are actually reading this book or just imagining that you're reading it. For example, if you dream that you're running, your mind can't tell whether you are actually running or just dreaming it. As a result, your body can react as if it were a real event by making you physically respond – you can sweat, breathe heavily or move your legs, and a sleepwalker may even get out of bed and run.

If you see a rope under your bed and are convinced it's a snake, then you will see a snake. If you are convinced that you won't like the taste of something even before you have tried it, then you probably won't like it. Someone who is frightened of spiders will see them in every corner, even when there are none.

On the other hand, if you're going to give a speech and you practise giving that speech by visualising yourself doing a great job in your mind, this 'pretend practice' will dramatically improve your actual performance.

The Tennis Match Test

Imagine you are at a tennis match, sitting mid-court, watching the ball being hit back and forth, back and forth, back and forth. Now, try that with your eyes closed. The result for most people is that their eyes will begin moving from side to side in their sockets to follow the imaginary ball. The mind doesn't know that you're not at a real tennis match and it makes your body respond as if the experience were real. This is precisely why visualisation works for achieving your goals.

Your brain can't tell the difference between reality and fantasy so it drives your body to try to fulfil the image you have imagined.

How sportspeople use visualisation

The visualisation technique has been practised for over 50 years in most sports and is now used by almost all Olympic athletes, whether they realise it or not. Sports psychologists instruct players to visualise themselves jumping the hurdles, catching a ball or hitting their target.

The world's top golf professionals know that one of the most important secrets of making a good golf shot is being able to visualise where you want the ball to go. They see in their mind the exact flight and path of the ball. If you can also hear the click of the ball and feel the smooth flex of your muscles, your chances of making the shot are high because the thought is fed through your RAS and into the neural networks in your brain. Your entire body chemistry receives the message clearly and knows what to do, and your muscles respond according to these exact instructions. Your timing, body control and swing come almost automatically because your visualisation has instructed your body what to do.

**'I never hit a shot – not even in practice –
without having a very sharp, in-focus picture
of it in my head.'
Jack Nicklaus**

Your mind thinks in pictures

Your mind does not think in words – it thinks in pictures. This is why your goals need to have crystal-clear descriptions, in writing. If, for example, you write as a goal 'I want to be rich', not much would happen because your mind can't imagine what that would look like. It's too vague and hazy. If, however, you write 'By 1 July 2020, I will own $1 million in net assets', your mind can now picture this scene and will begin searching for ways to achieve it. As mentioned earlier, if you state 'I want a beautiful home', your mind will have trouble picturing what it looks like because it's too hazy. If, however, you write a complete specification of your ideal home, right down to the exact type of door handles and paint colours, and then visualise yourself walking around this home, your mind will start searching for the resources necessary to get you there. This is why poverty is also a state of mind. People in poverty constantly visualise themselves having no money or opportunity and they keep affirming their circumstances. Anyone can be broke – most of us have been broke at times. But 'broke' simply means you have no money right now; you expect these circumstances to change soon. Poverty means constantly visualising never having anything at any time.

> **'If you are born poor it's not your mistake,**
> **But if you die poor it's your mistake.'**
> **Bill Gates**

Your goals, ideas and thoughts must be so vivid and precise that you are able to spell out every detail of them. You should be able to see not only your goals, but also every step you will take to reach them. And the way to achieve this kind of crystallised thinking is through the process of visualisation.

Worry is the result of visualising the things you don't want to happen – you visualise yourself dropping the ball, failing to clear the bar, the bank foreclosing your mortgage, or your partner leaving you for someone else. When you constantly visualise these things, your mind will create the circumstances that will fulfil the circumstances you have visualised.

This is why it is vital that you have a clear and positive picture of what you will achieve and where you will be when you have reached your goal. Visualise your desired outcome often and repetitively and your mind will begin to acknowledge it as normal, acceptable and achievable. Put all your passion and enthusiasm into imagining yourself when your goal is achieved.

Researchers Heather Kappes and Gabriele Oettingen found that only visualising the result of goals can sometimes be associated with occasional lack of momentum for some people. This is because the brain relaxes when it thinks it has achieved its goal. They suggest including critical visualisation in which obstacles, setbacks and other factors are also considered.

Evidence of how visualisation works

The power of visualisation was first discovered by Dr Edmund Jacobson, a pioneer in psychosomatic medicine. He had subjects visualise certain athletic activities and, through the use of sensitive detection instruments, he discovered subtle but very real movements in the muscles that corresponded to the movement the muscles would make if they were really performing the imagined activity. Further research revealed that a person who consistently visualises a certain physical skill develops 'muscle memory', which helps them when they physically engage in the activity.

A later well-known study by Australian psychologist Alan Richardson confirmed the reality of the power of visualisation. Richardson chose three groups of students at random. None had ever used visualisation. The first group practised basketball free throws every day for 20 days. The second made free throws only on the first day and the twentieth day. The members of the third group also made free throws only on the first day and the twentieth day but, in addition, they spent 20 minutes every day visualising free throws in their minds. If they 'missed' a shot, they 'practised' getting the next shot right, but only in their minds.

On the twentieth day Richardson measured the percentage

of improvement in each group. The group that practised daily improved 24 per cent. The second group, unsurprisingly, showed no improvement. The third group, which had physically practised no more than the second but had used visualisation, did 23 per cent better – almost as well as the first group.

In his paper on this experiment, published in *Research Quarterly*, Richardson wrote that the most effective visualisation occurs when the visualiser feels and sees what they are doing. In other words, the visualisers in the basketball experiment 'felt' the ball in their hands, 'heard' it bounce and 'saw' it go through the hoop.

**Mental practice has been shown to work
nearly as well as actual practice.**

Another study in 1995 found that adding visualisation practice into firearm training for police recruits was highly effective in improving performance. The visualisation group's marksmanship score resulted in an average gain of 32.86 points above the control group's score.

In 1954, Roger Bannister was the first person to run a mile in under four minutes. Before he broke this barrier, people believed that it was not physically possible for a human being to run a mile in that time. During his training sessions, Bannister repeatedly visualised himself running the mile in under four minutes. He reported that he did this so often that there were moments when he felt that he had already done it – his imagination had crossed the line into his perception of reality. Bannister eventually broke the four-minute-mile barrier because he believed that it was possible.

The 4-minute-mile was run another 26 times in the following year because when they realised that it was possible, other runners began to believe they could do it too. The RAS told their bodies what to do, which led to them achieve what was previously seen as impossible. The four-minute-mile barrier has since been broken thousands of times.

The discoveries of Carl and Stephanie Simonton

Doctors Carl and Stephanie Simonton – authors of the classic bestseller *Getting Well Again* – were pioneers in using visualisation techniques to stave off cancer and keep cancer patients alive and well. They conducted a study involving 245 people who had been diagnosed with advanced terminal cancer; 67 per cent were women and 33 per cent were men. The average age of those studied was 47. The therapy involved visualisation and relaxation skills practised for 10 to15 minutes, three times a day. It also employed other mental and emotional skills such as goal-setting, assertiveness-training, evaluating beliefs and identifying stress. The results they achieved confirmed beyond any doubt the power of the mind in keeping illnesses at bay.

The national median survival time in the United States then was 18 months for advanced breast cancer, compared to Simonton's result of 38.5 months. The national median survival time for advanced bowel cancer was 9 months, compared to Simonton's 22.5 months. National advanced lung cancer survival rates were 6 months – Simonton's were 14.5 months. These remarkable results were achieved purely by changing the images that patients were putting into their minds. No drugs, no chemo, no surgery or radiation, just filling the RAS with positive images and affirmations.

That is exactly why visualisation works so well for setting goals of any type. The one common 'skill' that stands out in almost every spontaneous remission case of cancer I have seen or known about is the use of meditation and visualisation. What you put into your mind is what you'll get.

I trained as a hypnotherapist in the 1970s (another of my goals was to be a stage hypnotist), and I created a stage act turning chief executives into chickens or getting them to sing like Elvis or walk like a duck. You feed into someone's mind that they are a rock star, and they can sing like never before. Tell them they are a police officer and they begin arresting people. And – as happened to me one evening – tell them they are a baby and they may pee in their pants! The basis of hypnosis is simple: if, under the right circumstances, your mind believes something, you can achieve it.

Other studies into 'Mental Rehearsal'

A study looking at brain patterns in weightlifters found that the muscle patterns activated when a weightlifter lifted hundreds of pounds were similarly activated when the lifters only imagined lifting.

Guang Yue, an exercise psychologist from Cleveland Clinic Foundation in Ohio, compared people who went to the gym with people who carried out virtual workouts in their heads. He found a 30 per cent muscle increase in the group who went to the gym, while those who only conducted mental weight-training exercises increased muscle strength by almost half as much (13.5 per cent). This average increase remained for three months following the mental training.

Matthew Nagle – who is paralysed in all four limbs – had a silicone chip implanted in his brain and used visualisation to transform his entire way of life. After just four days of mental practice, he could move a computer cursor on a screen, open emails, play a computer game, and control a robotic arm.

Natan Sharansky spent nine years in prison in the USSR after being accused of spying for the US. While in solitary confinement, he played himself in mental chess, saying, 'I might as well use the opportunity to become the world champion!' In 1996 Sharansky beat world champion chess player Garry Kasparov.

Can visualisation replace physical practice?

The simple answer is 'No'. A study conducted at the University of Chicago in 1960 compared the effect of mental practice with that of physical practice in the development of a motor skill. For this study, 144 students were separated into physical and mental practice groups on the basis of arm strength, intelligence and experience. Mental practice was found to be nearly as effective as physical practice under the conditions of this experiment. A 1994 analysis of 35 other related studies found that while mental practice was not as effective as physical practice, it proved to be a powerful way to improve actual physical performance.

A TRUE STORY : JIM CARREY

Comic actor Jim Carrey always believed he would have a bright future, even though he grew up in poverty and at one point his family was homeless and lived in a van. During his early teens he worked eight-hour shifts after school as a janitor. When Carrey was just starting out in Hollywood he was completely broke but, in a dramatic demonstration of visualisation, he wrote a cheque to himself for $10 million and dated it five years into the future. On the chequebook stub he wrote: 'For Services Rendered'.

He carried that cheque around in his wallet for years. Carrey would look at it every day and visualise having that money. He soon became one of the highest-paid entertainers in the industry, getting over $20 million per film.

**'Money isn't everything but it's better to cry
in a Mercedes than on a bicycle.'
Jim Carrey**

How to practise visualisation

Visualisation is simple, but it requires you to practise regularly to achieve the best results. Start with a simple skill that you want to master, like eating slowly, waking up early in the morning, or responding calmly to someone who usually bugs you. Starting with something easy strengthens your visualisation skills before tackling the bigger, more complex items.

Let's say, for example, you want to learn to play the guitar. Follow these steps:

1. Relax:
Find a quiet spot where nobody will bother you, close your eyes, take three deep breaths and let go of all tension.

2. Imagine what you will do:
Visualise the guitar, its shape, the strings and fingerboard

until you have a clear picture of it.

3. Put yourself into the picture:
Imagine picking up and holding the guitar. Notice how you sit with the guitar and add as much detail as possible.

4. Take action:
Feel the guitar in your hands, feel each string, and focus on the sound that each string makes. Start playing, just as you would in a practice session. Imagine yourself playing through several songs without stopping or missing a note, just as if you were an expert. When you have finished playing, open your eyes.

When you use visualisation, engage as many of your five senses as you can and imagine the scenes in as much detail as possible. For example, what are you wearing? Who are you with? What are you feeling right now? What do you hear and smell? What environment are you in?

Practise your visualisation early in the morning or just before you go to sleep at night. Imagine any roadblocks or hurdles you may encounter and see yourself successfully overcoming them.

Summary

Brain studies now reveal that thoughts produce the same mental instructions as physical actions. The strength of the mind–body connection and the link between thoughts and behaviours is well documented by science and is a vital connection for you in order to achieve the best from your life.

Visualisation has an impact on many of the functions in your brain, including motor control, attention, perception, planning and memory. This means that during visualisation your brain is being trained for actual performance. It's been found that visualisation enhances your motivation, increases your confidence and efficiency, improves your motor performance, and primes your brain for achieving your goals.

Research has also revealed that visualisation can be nearly as effective as physical practice, and that both together are more effective than either alone.

Begin by establishing a specific goal. Visualise that you have already achieved this goal and keep a mental image of it as if it were occurring to you right at that moment. Write a list of goals that you intend to visualise on the next page. You don't need to do them all today.

Visualisation works because it strengthens the neural pathways in your brain for any particular skill, and it will work for almost any goal you can set. Remember, your mind doesn't know the difference between actual events and visualised events. This means that you can practise your skill anytime or anywhere to help you improve. This is exactly the same way you have arrived at where you are in life right now, whether you have realised it or not. From today, only visualise the things you do want, not the ones you don't.

_____
_____
_____
_____
_____
_____
_____
_____
_____

And here is the quote with which we started this book:

**'Whatever the mind can conceive and
believe, the body can achieve.'
Napoleon Hill, 1937**

Chapter 8

The Power of Affirmations

Why what you say is what you'll get.

As well as visualising your goals, you also need to practise affirmations. An affirmation is any statement you regularly repeat to reaffirm to yourself what you intend to achieve or what you will do. An affirmation is a positive declaration of what you believe to be true, or the truth by which you choose to live. It's like an insurance policy for your goals and objectives – a type of declaration that you'll accomplish the things you want.

Like visualisation, affirmations travel through your RAS and rewire the neural pathways in your brain so the thought becomes a reality. Affirmations, therefore, are an essential way to change your internal thought patterns, your self-image and brain wiring, so that your goals will become your reality.

An affirmation is any saying or phrase that you listen to or repeat over and over until you eventually internalise it. In other words, it soon becomes a part of who you are.

For thousands of years philosophers, religious leaders, politicians and authors have used affirmations as a form of personal development or to motivate others to action. For example, Churchill's 'We shall fight them on the beaches' speech was an affirmation to motivate the British to overcome the enemy. John F. Kennedy's statement, 'Ask not what your country can do for you, ask what you can do for your country' was an affirmation to change American thinking. Muhammed Ali's 'I am the greatest' helped rocket him to becoming one of the world's most successful athletes. Affirmations help us express in words what we feel, and they reinforce the mission of the RAS to search for the circumstances we want. As we have said, your brain doesn't know the difference between reality and fantasy, and so affirmations work. As with visualisation, your brain accepts the affirmation as reality and creates the neural connections that drive your body toward your goal.

The use of affirmations is the key to constantly driving you forward toward the things you want, and is the process that top achievers everywhere use to help them accomplish their goals.

The key to making your own affirmations work is to choose the ones you want for yourself. Then visualise them and repeat them over and over until they become part of your being. It's that simple, and that is why what you say is what you'll get. The exciting thing about affirmations is that you have 100 per cent choice over which ones you put into your mind. And this is exactly the same process that negative thinkers use to get their lousy outcomes.

You can intentionally choose every affirmation you put into your mind.

What the sceptics think

Some people are sceptical about what we are saying here. They have difficulty accepting that what they say, over and over again, makes any difference to their outcomes. The truth is they have been practising negative affirmations for years. If someone continually says, 'I'm hopeless at remembering jokes' or 'I'm always late' or 'I never seem to finish anything I start' or 'I just can't make a speech in front of a group', they are practising negative affirmations and what they 'affirm' inevitably happens. Without even realising it, they think failure and live by it. With public speaking, if a person finds the courage to try to give a speech but says that they won't be any good, they screw it up badly, further confirming their negative affirmation. Conversely, if the person affirms that they can speak and repeats this and visualises it often enough, their RAS begins to believe they can do it. For example, if the person affirms, 'I can speak in public because I believe in what I say. I improve each time and my belief in my subject helps me be convincing to others. The more I speak, the more effective I become. Any mistakes I make are just stepping stones toward becoming an outstanding speaker', then this will become the reality.

If this all seems to you to be too good or too simple to be true, understand that it is the identical process to the way your current outlook on life was developed in the first place. No other person is responsible for your current circumstances. You created them with the help of your affirmations, whether you knew it or not.

Your affirmations summarise who you are.
What you say is what you get – good or bad.

A TRUE STORY FROM A READER – DARRIN CASSIDY

When I was young, I was keen on Kung Fu martial arts, but I was always having trouble with my spinning back-kick. I just couldn't do it, and I began to lose my confidence. The more I tried to do it the more I visualised how clumsy I was, and that made the clumsiness become my reality. Then one day I read about how basketball players stand in front of the hoop and imagine it being larger than it is and they visualise themselves dropping the ball into the hoop every time. I decided to visualise myself doing the spinning back-kick perfectly. I took a movie image of Bruce Lee performing the spinning back-kick and I played it over and over in my mind every day while I was at work. But instead of it being Bruce Lee, I changed the image to me.

Over three weeks I continued to visualise myself in that Bruce Lee movie performing that kick perfectly, and I repeated to myself over and over that my kick was getting better and better and how people were amazed at how well I could do it. But I didn't put any actual physical training into my kick during those three weeks – I only visualised it and continually affirmed what I wanted as the outcome.

When I finally made my first attempt after so much visualisation I actually pulled off a good spinning kick! It was exhilarating! It wasn't a brilliant first kick but it was damn good. My confidence then grew with each kick, and before I knew it my instructor had me demonstrating my kick for the class, and he even had me perform it at a public demonstration.

In later life, I suffered a crippling injury and I again used these same techniques to teach myself to walk again, through positive affirmations and visualisation. At the same time I set a goal to become a lawyer. I constantly visualised myself as a lawyer – like Tom Cruise in the movies Few Good Men *and* The Firm. *During my recovery time I also set a goal to earn a law degree and I was eventually admitted to the Bar. I discovered that if you constantly practise your visualisation techniques and repeat positive affirmations, there are no limits.*

How to frame an affirmation

State your affirmations in the positive. Remember, your mind can only think in positive images – it can't see something that isn't there. For an affirmation to work, it must be written and stated in positive terms so your mind can picture it. Your mind can't see an image connected with the words 'don't', 'won't' or 'can't'.

If someone tells a child, *'Don't fall off your bicycle'* their mind hears, *'fall off your bicycle'* and this can cause that to happen, whereas, *'I am becoming a good bicycle rider'* helps maintain balance.

Your mind can't see an image connected with the words 'don't', 'won't', or 'can't'.

In our world of ever-increasing obesity, humans have become obsessed with losing weight. If someone's goal is to lose weight, they may have affirmed, *'I'm going to lose 10 kilos'* or *'I'm not going to be fat any more'*, but they would also have found that it didn't work. Nothing changed because their mind couldn't picture a negative image.

The RAS simply can't see something that's not there. Their mind already has a picture of them carrying the extra kilos, so it creates the hunger feelings that drive that person to eat the things that will make their body match the heavier picture it holds of them. In other words, their mind – or self-image – is already programmed with a heavier picture of themselves.

Here's how to state a weight goal in the positive. Say, for example, you weigh 100 kilos, and want to lose 10 kilos, you could affirm, *'By 1 July, I will weigh 90 kilos.'* Your RAS now creates that image and your brain can imagine you as **being** 90 kilos as opposed to trying to see you **lose** 10 kilos.

Here's what to do

1. Start your affirmation with 'I am' or 'I will'.
For example, *'I am becoming a person who weighs 90 kilos'* or *'I will be 90 kilos by 1 July.'*

2. Be specific.
Unclear affirmations don't get results. For example, *'I am getting thinner'* does not have the power of *'I am becoming a person who weighs 90 kilos.'*

Many smokers say '*I will quit smoking*', but they rarely succeed. The RAS can't create a picture of taking something away or not doing something. If the smoker positively affirms '*I will become /I am a non- smoker*', the RAS can now create a picture of how a non-smoker looks, smells, dresses and behaves. Then it begins to motivate your body to match that image. The smoker will soon begin to lose the urge to smoke because the picture in their mind is of a person who has no craving for nicotine. It's that simple. It's not always easy, but it's that simple. Your RAS will always work for you when you program it correctly.

**Picture the results of what you do want –
not what you don't want.**

You can use positive affirmations for any goal or task. A study from the University of Michigan shows that seniors who have a positive attitude and use positive affirmations have a lower risk of heart failure than those who are pessimistic.

Am I just fooling myself?

You may think, *Just because I say it, it doesn't change reality*. While that seems true, repetition of your affirmations **does** change your perspectives about your life and these perspectives will eventually become your reality. Using our example of public speaking, let's say you constantly use a negative affirmation like *'I'm a hopeless public speaker'* and you are invited to stand in front of a group to give a speech. The research into human fears shows that the fear of public speaking is at the top of most people's list. Most people who are asked to give a speech imagine themselves as being fearful in front of an audience. People around them will reinforce this fear by saying things like, *'There's a jug of water for you beside the lectern'*, *'I hope it goes well'* or *'Good luck!'* These well-intentioned negative statements carry the subliminal message that they expect you to be fearful or nervous and to develop a dry throat, and that you'll need luck to give the speech because you probably won't do well.

When you are asked to take the stage your brain replays these affirmations and images like a film. It imagines you sweating, trembling, stuttering, forgetting your words and the audience being unimpressed. Your brain then causes your body to react to this mental picture as if it were true. Even if you are only dreaming that you are giving a speech, your body can respond with the same physical reactions as if you were actually doing it. Even an implied affirmation such as '*I don't like public speaking*', coupled with persistent repetition throughout your life, has a dramatic effect on your behaviour. If you believe you'll be fearful when speaking to an audience, your mind will make you fearful. If you believe you'll be confident and tell yourself this over and over, you will become more confident. That's how affirmations work.

A person's entire life is simply a collection of their affirmations.

Affirmations are the reasons why everyone's life is the way it is, and why we do or don't have certain things in our lives. Many people have been unconsciously collecting their affirmations throughout their lives and, for most of us, they work to our detriment. If you affirm '*I'm an idiot*', '*I'm not good at maths*', '*I can't make friends*', '*I'm hopeless at tennis/golf/squash*', '*I'm always getting lost*', '*I'm too old to start*' or '*That's just the way I am*', then these things will become your reality. It's not that they are real circumstances, but by being affirmed repetitively they became real.

The good news is that how you became the way you are today is the same process you can now use to get the things you really want. Even an implied affirmation – coupled with persistent repetition – has a dramatic effect on your behaviour.

'You are today where your thoughts have brought you; you will be tomorrow where your thoughts take you.'
James Lane Allen, American novelist

Try this simple speech test

Simple changes in your language can create a very different experience. Say the following three sentences to yourself out loud and notice how you experience each one:

1. '*I hope to enjoy my dinner tonight.*'
2. '*I want to enjoy dinner tonight.*'
3. '*I intend to enjoy my dinner tonight.*'

For most people, the first one will produce feelings of doubt. The second sentence will produce a different feeling. When you say, 'I want to enjoy dinner tonight' you will see what you want in the future, but you don't see yourself having it right now. The third statement of intending to enjoy your dinner puts you into the experience immediately. When you intend something to happen your RAS creates the experience of achieving your goal together with all the feelings, images and sounds that go with it.

**'You are a living magnet.
What you attract into your life is in harmony
with your dominant thoughts.'
Brian Tracy, entrepreneur**

The Displacement Principle

Affirmations work on the Displacement Principle. If you take a bucket filled with water and pour a cup of sand into it, the sand displaces an equal volume of water. The more sand you pour in, the more water is displaced. When the bucket is full of sand, there will be no water left because the sand has displaced it. In the same way, when you constantly feed a positive thought into your mind by an affirmation, you will displace a negative one. All you need to do is to continue to feed your mind positive affirmations by repetition until virtually all your original negative thoughts, doubts, fears and indecisions have been displaced.

Self-image

A self-image is a clear picture each of us holds of ourselves. It was largely created by the affirmations – both negative and positive – that our friends, family, society, religion and others have said about us and fed through our RAS. When we constantly reaffirm these affirmations to ourselves, they become the reality of who we now are. The RAS, however, can prevent our goals and positive messages getting through to our subconscious if our self-image is not congruent with our goals. That's why the Displacement Principle is so important. By constantly affirming the positive things you want, they will eventually replace the negative ones; they will become your new reality and your new self-image.

A TRUE STORY – SAM

When I was seven years old, my best friend was Sam. His mother constantly berated him in public. 'You're a very naughty boy' was one of her favourite affirmations about him, along with, 'You never get anything right' and 'The older you get, the worse you get!'

'He's always causing trouble,' she would tell her friends and family. Sam's father, however, saw him differently. He was proud of Sam – Sam was the apple of his eye. He would affirm, 'He's a little angel' and 'He'll make his mark in life – he's a really bright boy.'

Few people noticed that when Sam was around his father he was, in fact, a perfect angel and was very polite, just the way his father described him. When he was around his mother, however, he was the terror she expected him to be. Sam was living up to each of his parents' affirmations of him by acting out their expectations. When Sam was eight years old his father was killed in a car accident; after that Sam's mother raised him on her own. Her negative affirmations about him became more frequent and he lived up to every one of them. Before long he was affirming them to himself.

When he was 12 years old, he was asked to leave our school because he was 'undesirable'. His mother's negative affirmations about him became his reality. As a teenager, Sam was in and out of detention centres, living up to his mother's affirmation that he would 'become a menace to society'. At age 21 he was jailed for 3 years for drug-trafficking. On his release, he left Australia to become a mercenary in Africa and lived out his self-image of himself as a 'terrorist'. At age 27 he was killed in a gunfight in Nigeria.

This story is important because it shows how we will live up to the affirmations of our significant others, whether those affirmations about us are positive or negative.

Our parents, teachers, friends, relatives, partners and society will adversely affect our life when they program our RAS with negative affirmations about us. We also live up to the expectations that we have of ourselves and that we consciously or subconsciously repeat to ourselves with our daily affirmations.

You don't need to explain your affirmations to others – they'll probably tell you it doesn't work or to stop wasting your time and get a life.

Daydreaming versus affirmations

Having a list of affirmations is not the same as daydreaming. Daydreamers do not believe in their dreams. Their dreams are a whim or a fantasy that they probably would not even want to come true, even if it were possible.

Daydreamers never intend to take action on their dreams – they have no real plans or deadlines. Those who develop their powers of visualisation do so with a purpose.

Affirmations are not connected to willpower. Willpower is when you mentally or physically force yourself to do something. Affirmations are part of an overall plan to achieve a goal. They build the internal belief that you will achieve something.

You can choose every affirmation you put into your mind, and this is precisely why what you say is what you will get. Your RAS does not know the difference between reality and fantasy so it instructs your body to fulfil the affirmations you give it. This is also why, when you set positive goals with deadlines, you suddenly begin to see opportunities appearing everywhere. The way you behave, your attitude and even the way you talk begin to change. You literally start to become the new successful person you affirm yourself to be and to live up to your self-stated affirmations. What we say is what we get. This is also known as self-fulfilling prophecy.

> **'It's not what you say out of your mouth that determines your life, it's what you whisper to yourself that has the most power.'**
> **Robert Kiyosaki, American businessman and self-help author**

What happens when you say 'can't'?

It has been proven that when you think or say you can't do something, your brain decreases the amount of electrical energy going to the parts of your body that would be used to do the thing you claim you can't do. Try this simple test – hold your arm at 90 degrees to the side of your body, make a fist and think of something you can do really well. Now ask someone to try to push your arm down, and your task is to resist. Now, repeat this test but this time think of something you believe you *can't* do. You will discover that you will have difficulty resisting the person pushing down on your arm and that much of its prior strength will be gone. Your mind can't picture an image connected with the words 'can't', 'won't' and 'don't'.

A TRUE STORY – SCOTT'S AFFIRMATIONS

Scott decided to use affirmations to help him achieve several unlikely goals. 'Visualise what you want and write it down 15 times in a row, once a day, until you obtain it' was his approach. 'Within a few weeks, coincidences started to happen to me,' he reported. 'Amazing coincidences, strings of them, but within a few months the goal was accomplished exactly as I had written it.'

Scott then decided to pick another goal: to make some gains in the stock market. He wrote down his affirmation every day and then one night he woke up from a dream with the words 'Buy Chrysler' repeating in his head. He bought Chrysler shares during one of the company's most bleak periods, yet they began to rise soon after and he did well with the stock. He then wanted to get into the highly competitive MBA program at the University of California at Berkeley. He had already taken the GMAT (Graduate Management Admission Test) practice exams and had only hit the 77th per centile score.

He needed to be above the 90th per centile to have a shot at being accepted. He picked the target of hitting the 94th per centile on the GMAT as his goal and again applied his visualisation and affirmation techniques. He hit the 94th per centile and he graduated with a Berkeley MBA in 1986.

Soon, he set the 'crazy goal' – as his friends described it – of becoming a highly successful syndicated cartoonist.

In June 1996, Scott Adams' book The Dilbert Principle *became a number-one* New York Times *bestseller. In November his second book,* Dogbert's Top Secret Management Handbook, *also hit the bestseller list, giving Scott the number-one and number-two positions simultaneously.*

'Reporters often ask me if I am surprised at the success of the Dilbert comic strip. It definitely would be so, if not for my amazing experience with affirmations. I expected to achieve it.'
Scott Adams

Affirmations and cancer

Since my own diagnosis of cancer, I have met hundreds of people diagnosed with every type of cancer – lymphoma, breast, lung, liver, thyroid, oesophagus, ovarian, melanoma cancer – you name it, I've met it. Many of those whom I met or have counselled are now dead. I am often asked what the main differences were between those who lived and those who died, and there is one outstanding difference: the survivors made the decision to live, and took the necessary steps and action to achieve that goal. They used positive affirmations of what they intended to do with their lives.

Those who believed they would die, usually died. Sure, there are some positive-thinking survivors who died too and some negative thinkers who have survived, but as a group the survivors decided to live and those who died didn't make that decision. In over 20 years of cancer counselling, I have observed this phenomenon despite the type of cancer, the treatments or the prognosis patients receive. When you tell your RAS what to do, it does it – good or bad.

Summary

There are countless stories of people who have achieved their goals by using affirmations to focus their minds on their intended outcomes and who visualise their success ahead of time.

From today, every time you say something negative, restate it in a positive way. Goals must be *mind-accomplished* before they can become materially accomplished, and no-one can rise above their self-imposed limitations. Visualisation and affirmations can break down your own success barriers and set you free to achieve more creativity and untapped potential than you ever dreamed possible.

You can develop courage by affirming, '*I solve all problems by facing them head-on with courage and the conviction that I can overcome them.*'

Initiative can be developed with, '*I consider fatigue little more than boredom. I have an abundant supply of energy to draw upon when I choose.*'

Honesty can be developed by affirming, '*I am honest with myself and others at all times and under all circumstances*'.

Your life is the sum total of your past affirmations. When we practise affirmations, the Law of Reinforcement starts to work for us. First, we begin to look for those strengths and changes we have stated and to see in the real world the things we expect to see, just like Darrin did with his spinning back-kick, as Scott did with Dilbert and Sam did with his short life. We begin to act like the person we have resolved to be.

The way we walk and even our body language begins to change. Our conversation takes on the tone of a different person. We literally become a changed personality. And – like Darrin, Scott and Sam – we start to act the way we expect to act.

All successful athletes practise their sport both physically and mentally. Not only does a successful sprinter build their physical muscle by constant practice, they also have a picture of themselves winning each race. If athletes can't see and feel themselves crossing the finishing line in front of all other competitors, they stand little chance of winning. Always see yourself winning. What you tell yourself will happen.

**'The person who says, "I can!" and the
person who says "I can't!" are both right,
almost all of the time.'
Henry Ford**

Never think about what you *don't* want to happen. Only think about what you *do* want, regardless of the outcome of a situation. What you think about and what you affirm is what you'll usually get.

**An old man told his grandson, 'My son, there
is a battle between two wolves inside us all.
One is evil. It is anger, jealousy, greed,
resentment, inferiority, lies and ego. The other
is good. It is peace, hope, joy, love, humility,
kindness, empathy and truth.'**

**The boy thought about it and asked,
'Grandfather, which wolf wins?'**

The old man quietly replied, 'The one you feed.'

Chapter 9

Develop New Habits

Most people don't really want to hear the truth. They just want constant reassurance that what they choose to believe *is* the truth.

To operate at a high level of achievement and be successful there are certain habits you must learn and destructive habits you need to acknowledge and remove. For example, the most common habits that stop people from being successful include regularly eating junk food, not returning phone calls, forgetting people's names, not having a health and fitness routine, watching television, smoking, taking drugs or alcohol, always being late, and letting others abuse you. The habits of successful people include exercising at least three times a week, being on time for appointments, having a time-management plan, setting goals, returning calls, controlling finances, avoiding abusive people, and living a healthy lifestyle.

Over 80 per cent of all human behaviour is the result of habit – that is, behaviours we repeat over and over without having to think about them. This is important to us because if we had to make a conscious decision about every action we take – such as eating, brushing our teeth, dressing, driving, or our job – life would become stressful and overwhelming.

Repetitive habits allow us to walk and talk while brushing our teeth and to mentally plan our day while getting dressed.

How habits are formed

If you've ever seen a circus elephant, you may have noticed that only a light chain or rope is attached to its leg and a spike is driven into the ground to tether it. Any elephant would have no difficulty pulling the spike out or breaking a chain, yet fully grown elephants make no attempt to escape. So how does this happen?

When circus elephants are babies, one of their legs is shackled to a large block of concrete by a strong chain for hours every day. No amount of pulling, tugging, squealing or trumpeting will break that chain. As they grow older, they learn that however hard they try, it's impossible to break away. Eventually, they stop trying. They are now mentally conditioned to believe that when a chain is placed around their leg and tethered, it will be impossible to escape, no matter how light the chain or how it's anchored. When a chain is attached, they're mentally imprisoned.

From the day we are born, we are also conditioned by trainers. Apart from our hard-wired, natural instincts, we arrive in life with a blank mind and everything we think or do is a result of conditioning by our 'trainers' – our parents, siblings, friends, teachers, advertisements, society, religion, television, media and the Internet. Most of this conditioning is subtle and repetitive and enters our subconscious through the RAS, to be stored for decision-making at a later time. While some of this conditioning is designed to keep us safe, much of it stunts our personal growth. As a consequence, we also become imprisoned by mental and emotional chains.

Our parents tell us, '*Children are to be seen and not heard.*'
Our teachers tell us, '*Only speak when you're spoken to.*'
Our friends tell us, '*Never leave a secure job.*'
Society says, '*Pay off your mortgage and save for retirement.*'
Religions say, '*Obey the rules – or else.*'

Without realising it, most people allow these phrases to become the affirmations by which they live. The media constantly tell us we're not good enough. To be happy we must be slim, have perfect skin, shiny hair and white teeth, smell sweet, join a dating site, eat hamburgers, borrow money and drink lattes. Their messages are subtle and repetitive and become part of our belief system. As we grow through the formative years of our life, we are continually told what we can't do rather than what we can achieve. Just as the elephant is conditioned to believe it can't escape, we can easily become 'can't do' people. This negative, repetitive conditioning can hold us back from being successful.

You are confined only by the walls you build yourself.

Forming new habits

Most people have formed more negative habits than positive ones in their lives, so they respond to life's circumstances by continually repeating behaviours that either don't work or that get negative results. Most of these negative habits and attitudes are formed in childhood because the average 5-year-old child hears 'No' 11 times more than it hears 'Yes'.

Consequently, most people reach adulthood with a set of habits and attitudes that get them nowhere.

A typical 5-year-old hears the word 'Yes' 11 times a day and 'No' 121 times a day.

You are confronted every day by situations that need solutions, so developing positive habits that achieve the right results is critical to your success for every goal you set. Working out a way to deal with each circumstance lets you repeat positive behaviours that work each time you encounter an event or circumstance. This way, you don't need to make a conscious choice or decision each time something happens.

With repetition, your brain remembers what path it is necessary to take to deal with any given event and it goes into 'automatic mode'. This means you are not wasting time and energy trying to think of the right answer.

Thinking habits

Habits of thought are called 'attitudes'. These are more difficult to deal with than action habits because it's harder to nail down a single thought and to work on changing it. That's why writing your thoughts and attitudes on paper is so important: it lets you analyse each individual thought, each strand of your mental spaghetti ball. For example, in Cambodia eating grasshoppers, tarantulas, worms, cockroaches and other bugs is common, and this cuisine is even considered a delicacy. Few Western people have ever tried them, but most will have a definite attitude toward eating bugs, and it will be mostly negative. These attitudes are usually based on the association of bugs with possible diseases, and not on the nutritional value of the insects. When my son Brandon and I were in Siberia, our hosts served us a meal that included ox tongues, pig's feet, cow's eyes, sheep's brains and other unidentifiable delicacies. Most non-Siberians would shrink with fear at the thought of eating a meal like this and might even begin to feel ill as their RAS is given a picture of them consuming it.

But if you think only about the nutritional value of such a meal you can deal with eating it – and so we did. Achieving anything in life begins with feeding your RAS the positive images of what you want.

**A bad attitude is like a flat tyre.
You can't go anywhere until you change it.**

Most people have trouble changing negative habits because they only try to alter the physical actions associated with the habit rather than its root cause – the thought. You could easily use a fork to scoop up and eat sheep's brains, but without first changing your attitude to why you should do so it will not become a permanent habit.

Enthusiasm, self-respect, determination and confidence are all habitual, positive ways of thinking, just as procrastination, denial and complaining are habitual, negative ones.

Self-confidence is a habit of thought. Confidence means you know that the course of action you are taking will give you a positive result. But acquiring that knowledge can only come from your having attempted to do something a number of different ways and finding the right way for you. And most attempts at new things usually don't produce immediate good results. This is why failure is a vital part of success: the more you fail, the more you will learn the right way to go, and the more self-confident you will become. The person who has never failed has never achieved anything. And most people are afraid of failure so they never attempt much.

'Failure is a prerequisite for great success. If you
want to succeed faster, double your rate of failure.'
Brian Tracy

Be consistent

Productive and successful people constantly practise the
things that are important to them. The best weightlifters are
in the gym at the same time every week. The best writers are
sitting at their keyboard every day. This principle applies
to the best leaders, parents, managers, musicians and
doctors. For top performers, it's not about the performance,
it's about continual practice.

A typical loser's bad habit list usually includes:

Letting people get under their skin
Procrastinating
Not keeping a diary
Talking too much and not listening
Always running late
Eating junk food
Avoiding fitness regimes
Stressful relationships
Financial problems
Being unhappy
Being the Fun Police
Being in a job they hate.

To develop new, productive habits, you first need to write a list of all the non-productive habits you currently have. Ask friends and colleagues to help you if you are unsure. If you are really stuck, ask your relatives – they'll be quick to give you a long list.

The most common negative phrases

Few people realise that phrases such as *'I'll try'* and *'I don't have time'* or *'I'm too busy'* are all habitual negative affirmations that losers use.

'I don't have time' is the grown-up version of 'the dog ate my homework'. 'I'll try' is used by habitual under-achievers who announce, in advance, that they don't expect to succeed at a task. 'I'm too busy' reveals that a person is disorganised, or that your request is unimportant to them.

**No-one is ever 'too busy' –
it's all about priorities.**

You can replace negative thought habits and attitudes with a simple three-step technique:

1. *Acknowledge that you have a negative habit*
2. *Determine the source of the habit*
3. *Develop a new, positive habit and use the displacement principle to replace the negative one.*

If you think hard enough about a negative habit you may have acquired, you can usually figure out where it came from. To change a thought habit, write down your new thought habit and feed it into your RAS using visualisation and affirmations to make it become permanent. It's simply a matter of replacing one way of thinking with another. This is the same process that people used to develop their negative habits in the first place.

As a guide, here are some of the usual habits of successful and unsuccessful people

Successful people	Unsuccessful people
Compliment others	*Criticise others*
Forgive others	*Hold grudges*
Encourage others to succeed	*Hope others will fail*
See the funny side of things	*Get upset about things*
Are thankful	*Feel entitled to things*
Talk about ideas	*Talk about people*
Read regularly	*Watch TV every day*
Have a 'to-do' list	*Make it up as they go*
Keep learning	*Think they know it all*
Credit others	*Take all the credit*
Accept responsibility for failures	*Blame others*
Share information and ideas	*Keep it all to themselves*
Expect and embrace change	*Fear change*
Have plans and set goals	*Have no plans or goals*

Circle or tick any of the habits on the right as some of your own, and use the corresponding habits on the left to displace them.

Get new friends

Like it or not, you will become the average of the five people you hang out with the most. If you are the most successful person in your group of friends, there will be a silent, constant pressure from the others that gradually pulls you back to the average of the group's income, achievements, possessions and attitudes to life.

Conversely, the least successful person in the group benefits most by being gradually pulled up to the group average. Your parents understood this principle, and this is why they constantly tried to keep you away from the kids they considered 'no good' or from 'the wrong side of the tracks'.

So when it comes to friends, choose carefully. Decide now to surround yourself with people who have achieved what you want to achieve, or who are going in the direction you want to go. You can't hang around with negative people and live a positive life. This doesn't mean you dump your old friends. It simply means that you accumulate new friends whose influence can help raise you to your next level.

The best way to improve is to surround yourself with better people.
They will make you a better person.

Here's what to do now: write a list of the names of everyone in your life with whom you spend time. Include family members, co-workers, neighbours and old school friends. Next, put a tick beside the names of those people who have a positive influence on your life, those who encourage you to do better and who themselves are moving forward. Now put a cross beside the names of those who are negative, say it can't be done, criticise you, blame others for everything, are jealous of you or always tell you how bad things are.

Next – stop spending time with the people with the crosses beside their names! If that's difficult (because they live in the same house as you, for example), reduce your involvement with them. You don't have to spend time with negative people just because you have known them a long time or are related to them. It doesn't mean you don't love them any less, just don't waste your time listening to their negative crap. For example, if someone creates stress in your life by being around you or just by calling you on the phone, or if they want to stamp on your goals or dreams, stop wasting your time with them.

Stay away from negative people, toxic people, dream-stealers and emotional vampires.

A TRUE STORY: MICHELLE AND GAIL

Gail would call Michelle regularly to gossip about people, talk about how bad her life was, how all men are bastards and that the future was grim. Michelle regularly offered Gail advice on how to make things better, but Gail never took any of it. These phone calls usually lasted for over an hour and they always left Michelle feeling negative or depressed. Michelle often became short-tempered with her children, and her libido sometimes disappeared for weeks because of the calls.

Michelle used our list technique and marked a cross beside Gail's name. This was difficult because they were cousins. You see, Gail had been using Michelle as a whipping boy under the guise of 'genetic obligation'. In other words, 'You're related to me so you are obliged to listen to my crap.' Michelle decided to ask her husband to answer the phone on the nights when Gail would call, and he was to say that Michelle was unavailable or was out. On the occasions when Michelle inadvertently got caught on the phone with Gail, she would stop herself giving advice and would change the subject when Gail started her negative talk.

Within two months, Gail had stopped her negative phone assaults on Michelle and was calling other unlucky family members instead. Today, Michelle and Gail get on better than ever when they meet at family events because Gail realises that Michelle will no longer allow herself to be used by emotional vampires.

Be with people who bring out the best in you, not the stress in you.

Many people stay with the wrong life partner just because they have been together for a long time, claiming they stay because they have 'history together' or 'for the sake of the children' when they are, in fact, being poor role models for their children. Others put up with negative family members simply because they are related to them. Time or genetics doesn't make you an indentured servant to someone and there is no such thing as 'genetic obligation'. If you want to move forward with your life and you've put a cross beside someone's name on your list, limit or stop your interaction with them. This idea is controversial for some people but remember, if your current five closest friends aren't encouraging you to improve your life, they are probably draining you or holding you back. We are not saying you shouldn't have a wide range of friends – we are saying that you will become the average of the five people you hang out with the most. If you don't like that average, change things. And once you free yourself from negative people, positive ones will appear.

If you hang around five millionaires, you will become the sixth one. If you hang around five broke people, you will become the sixth one.

Some people will debate this affirmation about millionaires and broke people. Close analysis of the pessimists, however, will reveal that they are the broke people who hang around with other broke people. You can't hang around with negative people and expect to get positive results in your life.

As you improve yourself and move forward to better things, try to avoid the cynics and dream-stealers and those who have a victim mentality or dwell in mediocrity until you are confident enough to deal with the constant procession of crap-throwers you will encounter in life. Make a conscious decision to surround yourself with positive, uplifting people who encourage you to go where you want to go and who will applaud you when you get there.

A bird sitting in a tree is never afraid of the branch breaking because its trust is not in the branch but in its own wings.

Summary

Good habits will give you positive results. Poor habits will give you more of the negative stuff you've been getting from life. You always have almost complete control over your choice of thoughts and habits.

In simple terms, intentionally acquiring the habits of successful people will lead you to the success you want. Holding on to non-productive habits is a millstone around your neck that prevents you from moving forward. Your eventual success – or not – in any venture will be controlled by your learned, habitual thoughts and attitudes.

Take one non-productive habit at a time and develop a plan for replacing it with a positive one. Make a pact with yourself never again to go into a fast-food outlet. This will force you to look for healthy alternatives that are always available when you put yourself in a position of having to find them. Decide to run your business life by a diary and keep it with you at all times. Buy a book on how to remember people's names. If you smoke, drink or take drugs, take the necessary steps to quit now.

Avoid the habit of hanging out with people who impede your success. If you are not thrilled by the lifestyle and achievements of your closest five friends, find new ones. To find these people, ask yourself where your new friends currently hang out. What clubs, associations, schools or organisations do they belong to? Join those organisations and volunteer to be on a committee. Then, very quickly, you'll accumulate new friends who are already where you want to be. If you merely stay with your current group of friends you can only expect to continue to achieve the average of that group. Many people feel compelled to spend time with friends they went to school with, once worked with or are related to. That's fine provided you are prepared to be part of the average of who they are and what they have in life. If you don't want to be the average of your current friends, find new ones.

Your current life habits and attitudes are like water in a bucket that has mostly been filled by parents, teachers, peers, society and the media.

Each new skill and positive approach you learn from this book is like a cup of sand that will eventually displace most of the bad habits. Your bucket will then be full of the positive skills, attitudes and habits that will take you to where you want to go. Select one skill each week and practise it until it becomes a part of who you are. It takes 30 days of repetition to form a new habit and to make it permanent. Start *now* to replace negative restraints with positive habits. You can achieve this in the same way the circus elephant was trained – by repetitive learning.

Continually practise *positive* actions until they become 'can do' habits.

▼

For the rest of your life, make a habit of setting daily goals and achieving them. Focus on the things you want, not the things you don't want.

Chapter 10

Play the Numbers Game

**An accountant was nervous about flying so he
rang the Bureau of Statistics and asked,
'What are the odds of getting on a plane from
Sydney to London that has a bomb on board?'
The Bureau said the chances were about one in
two million. 'I want better odds!' he demanded.
So they asked the computer for better numbers.**

**'We suggest you take a bomb on board with you,'
they told him, 'because the odds of boarding
a plane that has two bombs is only
one in fifteen million.'**

Most people complain about how busy they are, whether it's with work, family, or just the basic upkeep of life. Yet there are others who have exactly the same amount of time who do remarkable things. Most people also think that successful people probably worked harder, got lucky or were in the right place at the right time and therefore made it further than them. But that is not the truth. So how do the high achievers do it?

Every activity you undertake in life has a mathematical set of principles, laws and ratios attached to it. The answer is to discover the numbers and ratios that apply to a given event and to use this information to propel you forward. This chapter will show you the most important numerical laws you need to know.

The Law of Averages

This law governs the success of every activity in life. It means that if you do the same thing over and over, under the same circumstances, you will achieve a set of results that will remain constant. This law was the one we revealed in our bestselling book *Questions are the Answers*.

To demonstrate how the Law of Averages works, let's assume that the average payout on a poker machine is 10:1. On a $1 poker machine it means that, on average, every ten times you insert $1 and spin the wheels you will receive a win of between 60 cents and $20. Your statistical chance of having a win between $20 and $100, however, is only 118:1. There is no real skill involved because the machines are programmed to pay out on pre-set ratios. Just as these machines are programmed to pay based on statistical averages, so does every other thing you undertake in your life. And these are the numbers you need to know.

When I was selling life insurance, I learned a statistic of 1:56. It meant that if you approached everyone on the street and asked, '*Would you like to buy some life insurance?*' one in 56 would answer '*Yes*'. This meant that if all I ever did was to ask that question 168 times a day I'd make three sales a day and would be in the top 5 per cent of all insurance salespeople! If you stood on a street corner and asked every passer-by to help you get your ideas off the ground, perhaps only one in 50 would agree to help you, maybe more, maybe less.

When I was 11 years old, I sold rubber sponges door-to-door for 20 cents each. My averages were 10:7:4:2.

This meant that for every ten doors I knocked on after school between 4 p.m. and 6 p.m., on average seven residents would answer the door. Four would listen to my practised presentation and two would buy a rubber sponge; this meant I made 40 cents. I could usually knock on up to 30 doors in an hour, so I'd average 12 sales for the 2 hours and I'd make $2.40. In 1962, this was a lot of money for an 11-year-old Australian kid. My father was a life insurance salesman and had taught me about the Law of Averages, so when I went out after school I knew that for every 10 doors I knocked on, I'd earn 40 cents. I never worried about the 3 in 10 doors that didn't open, or the three people who wouldn't listen, or anyone who told me to go away, or even the two people who said 'No'. All I knew was that if I knocked on 10 doors, I'd make 40 cents. This meant that every time my knuckles knocked on a new door, I'd make 4 cents, regardless of what happened next.

This was a powerful, motivating force for me – knock on 10 doors and earn 40 cents! So success was simply a matter of how quickly I could knock on ten doors and attempt my presentation.

Most people don't know about the Law of Averages and so they are motivated by **what happens to them next**. And, statistically speaking, 80 per cent of what you do in your attempt to achieve anything will produce *nothing*. While my ratio of 10:7:4:2 produced two sales and I earned 40 cents, 80 per cent of my overall activity still produced zero. But just like a poker machine, I knew that if I spun the wheels 10 times, I'd get the 40 cents even if most of my spins produced nothing. This is why you must talk to everyone about your ideas, plans and goals and ask them to help you or to advise you or to participate. Play the numbers game. Statistically, at least one in five people who know you will be willing to help you. Having a secret desire is a nice idea, but you must ask those who can help you to do so.

Do you have a secret goal or desire? If so, how long will you keep it a secret?

Whatever your goal, there is a ratio – a set of numbers – that determines how many times you attempt it and how many times you will succeed. It's simply a matter of discovering those numbers. The reason people become despondent when trying to move forward with their goals is because they don't understand this first law. They are motivated by what happens next and, as we've said, most of what happens next will not produce a result. Most successful salespeople understand this law, but it also applies to every activity you undertake. You just need to figure out your personal numbers.

As a teenager I had a job after school, selling pots, pans, linen and blankets by referral and cold-calling. Again, I used the Law of Averages. After 30 days I calculated my ratio to be 5:3:2:1.

It meant that for every five prospective customers I would call on the telephone, three would agree to see me. I would make a presentation to only two of them because the third one either stood me up, cancelled the appointment, wouldn't listen or had some other objection beyond my control, such as they were unemployed or broke, people were arguing in the next room, a dog bit me or the building I was in was hit by lightning (these things actually happened to me).

Of the two prospects who listened to my presentation, one would buy and I'd make $45. This meant that every time I spoke to five prospects on the phone, it would eventually result in $45 commission. So every time I spoke with a prospect on the phone, I'd make $9! It didn't matter whether a person agreed to see me or not, whether they turned up or not, or even if they said 'Yes' or 'No'. As long as I attempted to make an appointment over the phone, I'd end up with $9 each time someone answered it. So I drew a big sign with '$9' written on it and put it beside my telephone. Before long, I was the number-one pot and pan salesman in Australia.

At age 20, I joined the big time of professional selling – life insurance. I quickly established my ratio to be 10:5:4:3:1.

For every ten prospects I called, five would agree to an appointment and one didn't keep it, so I'd actually get to eyeball four prospects. I'd present to three and would sell to one, making $300 commission. This meant that every time I spoke to someone on the telephone I would earn $30, regardless of whether they agreed to see me, or kept the appointment, or voiced objections or bought from me or not. My focus was never on looking for buyers – it was on calling ten prospects every day as my number-one priority, and that was fairly straightforward. Playing the numbers is a more important step than making the sales.

> **Sales people don't fail because of the prospects they don't sell, but because of the prospects they don't see.**

By age 21 I drove a Mercedes-Benz, owned my own home, lived a fabulous lifestyle and was the youngest person in Australia ever to qualify for the Million Dollar Round Table in the USA. Using the Law of Averages, by age 24 I had qualified for the international top 20 salesmen with one of Australia's largest insurance companies. At age 28 I forged a partnership with Australia's wealthiest man, Kerry Packer, and cricket legend Tony Greig. We built Australia's largest independent insurance brokerage using television prospecting. And the key to all these successes was the understanding of how numbers and ratios work.

The 80/20 Principle

This is one of the most compelling statistical rules you will ever learn, and the great thing about it is that you don't have to be a statistical genius to make it work for you.

The 80/20 Principle is also called the 'Pareto Principle', after the Italian economist Vilfredo Pareto, who observed that 80 per cent of Italy's income was received by 20 per cent of the Italian population. This principle says that most of the results in any situation are determined by a small number of causes. The numbers mean that 80 per cent of your outcomes come from 20 per cent of your inputs. The important point to understand is that in your life there are certain activities you do (your 20 per cent) that account for the majority (the 80 per cent) of your happiness, results and outputs. This is why, if you were to analyse the time you spend on activities in any given week, you'd find that most of them have very little impact on anything that happens.

Over 80 per cent of the world's wealth is owned by less than 20 per cent of the world's population.

You can apply the 80/20 Principle to almost anything. For example, in business, 20 per cent of inventory on hand occupies 80 per cent of the warehouse space. Similarly, 80 per cent of the inventory line items come from 20 per cent of the vendors. It's typical that 80 per cent of a company's revenue will be the result of sales made by 20 per cent of the sales staff. Twenty per cent of employees are responsible for 80 per cent of a company's output, or 20 per cent of customers are responsible for 80 per cent of the revenues. And while 20 per cent of workers will cause 80 per cent of company problems, another 20 per cent of personnel will deliver 80 per cent of the entire production. And 20 per cent of product defects cause 80 per cent of product problems. Most project managers know that 20 per cent of work (usually the first 10 per cent and the last 10 per cent) consumes 80 per cent of the available time and resources. For most people, there are usually only a handful of activities they perform each week that produce their income. In other words, 20 per cent of their activities produce 80 per cent of their financial rewards.

When you analyse the distribution of wealth and resources in the world, you will discover that a small percentage of the population controls the biggest chunk, clearly demonstrating the 80/20 rule. You can also apply the 80/20 rule to your overall happiness and satisfaction in most situations in life.

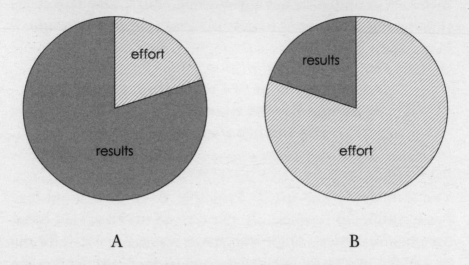

A

B

A. How successful people use the 80/20 Principle.
B. How most people use the 80/20 Principle.

The 80/20 Principle constantly demonstrates that in most things you do, 80 per cent of your results come from 20 per cent of your efforts. It also means that for most people, 20 per cent of their results come from 80 per cent of their efforts. These are not hard-and-fast rules and not every activity will always be exactly 80/20, but when you look at many key factors in most things, there is usually a minority creating a majority.

By recording your daily habits and analysing them you will find many examples where the 80/20 rule applies to you. You probably make most of your phone calls to a very small percentage of the people for whom you have phone numbers, and you probably spend most of your time with only a few people from all those you know. You likely spend a large amount of your money on a few things – rent, mortgage payments and food.

Most people will discover that much of their time is spent procrastinating or working inefficiently, doing activities that provide very little benefit. And most people spend 80 per cent of their time working in jobs they hate to make enough money to enjoy the other 20 per cent of their time.

Procaffeinating – (n.) the tendency not to start anything until you've had a cup of coffee.

From a business standpoint, finding the 80/20 ratio is vital for maximising your performance. You need to identify the products, services or actions that generate the most income – the 20 per cent – and drop the rest – the 80 per cent – that provide minimal results. Spend your time working on the things that you can improve significantly with your core skills and leave the other 80 per cent to other people. Work hardest on the things that give you the best results. Reward the best employees and phase out the worst. Drop the bad clients and focus on upselling and improving service to your best clients.

The 80/20 Principle is a constant reminder that only 20 per cent of all the tasks you do during the day really matter. They will likely produce 80 per cent of the results, so focus mainly on those things.

If you are getting caught up in a daily crisis, remember that the critical 20 per cent is what you need to focus on.

If you can tweak your activity to focus on the actions that really matter, you can live an amazing life. By eliminating 80 per cent of all your hard work you can take the remaining 20 per cent and achieve outstanding results. And that's what highly successful people do.

As we showed in Chapters 2 and 3, the first thing you must do is determine what you are passionate about. To start living an 80/20 life right now, you need to focus your energies on your passions. If you think your life lacks direction or you feel depressed, it's because you haven't clearly identified your passions. Once you have done so, you can start immediately applying the 80/20 rule to your life. Many people do a full-time job and work after hours on a business, a hobby or their creative talent. If this is you, then your ratio is not 80/20; it is probably more like 20/80. You are probably spending too much time at a job you don't like and so you are not motivated to do it well. You aren't in the 80/20 'effective employee' category that your company wants. When you get home at night you are probably too exhausted to spend time on your passion and you feel like you are getting nowhere. This is a lifestyle where your actions fall into the 80 per cent that produce 20 per cent of your happiness. You are getting very little out of your life and the people you work for are getting very little from you. Everyone loses.

If you are spending 80 per cent of your time doing something you don't like, quit.

If this describes you, start changing your ratios. Reduce the amount of time you spend on the activities you don't like and increase the amount of time you spend on your passion. You may say you can't do this because you need the money – but most people don't need as much money as they think they do. Most people can live off part-time work, but they choose to work more because they want to buy more materialistic things. We're not saying you need to live in poverty, but you know that your real happiness comes from doing the things you enjoy most, including spending time with your family, not from earning more money. Chasing money for money's sake doesn't work.

Are you really living your life or are you just paying bills until you die?

Chasing your passion often leads to a greater income because the quality of your output is much higher. Focus your energy on increasing time invested in your core strengths and the rewards will follow. Reduce your working hours each week and spend more time attracting clients to your next business, booking more music gigs, writing your book, developing your invention or software program, or finding investors to buy shares in what it is you really want to do. If you aren't interested in turning your passions into income, what we suggest here is still a good option for you.

If money isn't your primary concern but your music is, for example, then why spend so much time working to earn more money than you need? Sure, you should plan for the future and build assets, but don't let this take up all of your time and energy. It won't satisfy your musical soul. You can be happy without a mansion by the sea, and if you spent more time on your music the potential album sales may one day lead to it. At worst, you will be much happier when you follow your enthusiasm rather than following money.

> **'Most people die with their music still in them because they are always getting ready to live. Before they know it, time runs out.'**
> **Oliver Wendell Holmes, Associate Justice of the Supreme Court of the United States**

If financial freedom is important to you and a big part of your plans, then start to convert your passions into income-generating ideas. Grow your business step by step, client by client, gig by gig, song by song or sale by sale. Keep adjusting your work/passion time ratio as your business grows to support you and you no longer need the income from your job.

> **Look for 80/20 activities in everything you do and drop any tasks that don't produce results. Focus on what really matters and let go of what doesn't.**

How most people play the numbers game

The most common approach to playing numbers is the lottery, but the statistical odds of success are so remote that wealthy people don't participate. Lotteries everywhere promote the illusion that when you win, all your problems will be solved and you will live happily ever after. The statistics, however, tell a different story. In the USA, for example, seven out of eight lottery winners are broke within seven years, half of them file for bankruptcy within four years and their suicide rate is three times the national average. So what happened?

Lottery winners are mostly working-class people. When they win they typically move to a classier neighbourhood, buy a big house and a new car. Unfortunately for most lottery winners, however, few of their new neighbours identify with them and so the winners have difficulty in making new friends. Their former friends reject them: they can't communicate with them any more because money gets in the way. After three years, lottery winners are 30–40 per cent fatter than the rest of society and they begin to die earlier. The people who buy almost all lottery tickets and win most of the money usually have little to no experience in handling large amounts of money – and so they blow it.

Seven out of eight lottery winners in the USA are broke within seven years, half of them file for bankruptcy within four years and their suicide rate is three times the national average.

Similar statistics apply to people who inherit large amounts of money or who receive large settlements from a court case. Sometimes, lottery winners will make a media splash about their windfall and then have to move away because of persistent harassment from charities and con artists. Studies show that lottery winners who receive smaller wins – up to $500,000 – can improve their lives and do better if they seek competent financial planning advice. However, most don't do this. They typically take advice from well-meaning friends and relatives who are not financially successful themselves – and lose it. Give the winners $10 million or more, however, and the statistics reveal that you will give them a life of misery, no friends, poor health and early death. As a group, wealthy and highly successful people are least likely to buy lottery tickets because they feel the odds of winning are too low and they would rather take responsibility for financial outcomes rather than leave things to chance.

When you set clearly defined financial goals and have a plan of action with a deadline, your odds of winning are far greater than any lottery payout or financial windfall. And most importantly, your own goals put you in the driver's seat of your financial life.

My therapist placed half a glass of water in front of me. He said that if the glass was half full, I was an optimist. If it was half empty I was a pessimist. So I drank the water and told him I was a problem solver.

The top 3 per cent

I was diagnosed with aggressive prostate cancer at the age of 47. The future looked grim for me. After my second round of surgery I was lying in a hospital bed, high on morphine and with 13 tubes pumping things in and out of me when a specialist walked into the room and told me calmly that I had a 'positive margin'. That's medical talk for 'the cancer got out and is running around somewhere in your body'. Another specialist came to explain the next proposed course of treatment – radiation. They wanted to cook my ass in a microwave oven. Everything has a set of numbers so I asked, 'What are my odds if I don't do it?'

'You'll live for about three years,' one of the specialists answered. 'The first two years should be okay but the last year is not so good…'

I asked him to explain what he meant.

'Well, if we take a hundred men your age in your condition, about 20 per cent would die within two years and about 50 per cent within three years. Most of the rest would die soon after that.'

'Does anyone survive?' I asked.

'About 3 per cent will live past eighty and die of something else,' he calmly replied.

'Well, Doc,' I said, 'I'll take the 3 per cent group!'

He looked at me quizzically. 'I'll be in the 3 per cent who live past age eighty,' I announced. 'What do I need to do to qualify?'

'That's not how it works!' he said. 'These are the statistics for men in your condition at your age. You don't choose your group!'

What? Why not? Someone had to be in the 3 per cent

group, so why couldn't it be me? The specialist agreed that someone would be in the 3 per cent, but it wasn't for me to choose it. It was just a statistical number. I then explained to him why he had it wrong, not me. Clearly, the survivors in the 3 per cent group were doing something that the other 97 per cent weren't. So what was it?

Not only did he not know what the 3 per cent were doing, but I could also see he didn't understand the idea that you can choose your group.

I soon discovered that the doctors didn't know how anyone could make it into the top 3 per cent. Most simply ignored my question as if I were an idiot. But to me it was simple – some people have to be in the top 3 per cent and I decided to be one of them. I just needed to know what I had to do to qualify.

I decided that life-threatening cancer was simply another one of the obstacles that stood in the way of the things Barb and I wanted to do. I spent the next year searching out the people who were in the 3 per cent group and studied what they were doing and why they were still alive. I was going to move that obstacle. I became a chemical-free, non-drinking, organic vegetarian and I lived every bit of advice in this book. That was 16 years ago. Everything in life has a set of numbers – you just need to find out what they are.

Summary

It doesn't matter what activity or venture you undertake in life, including finding the perfect partner or surviving an illness, each one has a set of statistics – a ratio – attached to it. You also have a personal set of statistics that will determine your odds of success. These numbers will show you the areas where you need to improve your skills to give yourself the best odds at whatever you attempt. Ratios tell you where to best spend your time and what activities you should avoid.

All you need to do is to record all your daily activities, such as how many times you attempted something, how often you succeeded or failed, what achieved a result and what did not. Soon your ratios will appear.

Discover what your real passions are and write them down below in clearly defined descriptions. Remove money from the equation so that you can think without worrying about finances, and make plans to move toward 80/20 lifestyle activities.

Maximise what you are good at. Find the activities that produce the most results for you in your business and personal life and put your energy where the big rewards are.

Don't waste your time on 'get rich quick' schemes and your hard-earned money on lotteries.

When you understand your numbers, the roads to success become clearer.

The Answer

Chapter 11

Dealing with Stress

Successful people everywhere share one trait in common – they have learned to see the funny side of negative events. There's a positive, humorous aspect to every negative thing that can happen in life – you just have to look for it. The study of humour and laughter and its psychological and physiological effects on the human body is called *gelotology*.

Think of the last time someone told you a really great joke that made you buckle up with laughter and you couldn't control yourself. How did you feel afterwards? You felt a tingle all over, right? Your brain had released a chemical called endorphin into your blood system, which gave you what has been described as a 'natural high'. In effect, you were temporarily 'stoned' when you laughed long and hard.

Those who have trouble with laughing at life often turn to drugs and alcohol to achieve that 'stoned' feeling. Alcohol loosens inhibitions and lets people laugh, which in turn releases endorphins. This is why most well-adjusted people often laugh more when they use drugs and alcohol, and unhappy people may become even more miserable or even violent.

At the end of a big laughter session you will sometimes say, 'I just laughed until I cried!' Tears contain encephalin, one of the body's natural tranquillisers, which relieves pain. We cry when we experience a painful event and endorphins aid self-anaesthesia.

A new study has found that women with large butts live longer than men who mention it.

The science behind laughter

Laughter is similar among other primates including gorillas and orangutans, indicating that laughter appears to have a common origin among primates. Its biological origins are as a type of shared expression of relief at the passing of danger. Laughter research shows that parts of the brain's primitive limbic system (this controls basic emotions such as fear, pleasure and anger) are involved in laughter and emotions, and help us with the basic functions necessary for survival.

The sound of laughter is caused by the epiglottis constricting the larynx, causing respiratory sounds. So it's a modified form of breathing. The two structures in the limbic system involved in producing laughter are the amygdala and the hippocampus.

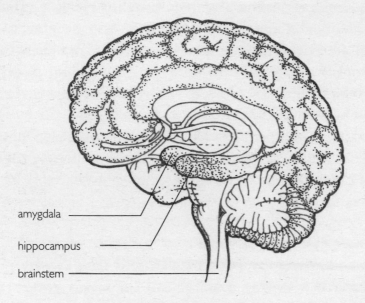

amygdala

hippocampus

brainstem

Where laughter sits in the brain.

A positive link has been found between laughter and the function of blood vessels. Laughter causes the tissues that form the inner lining of blood vessels, the endothelium, to dilate or expand to increase blood flow. The ventromedial prefrontal cortex produces the endorphins that enter your bloodstream and make you feel happy when you laugh.

Okay, so much for the not-very-funny technical stuff.

How humour and jokes work

The basis of most jokes is that something disastrous or painful happens to someone. Even though we consciously know that the punchline of the joke is not a real event, the joke is fed through the RAS and, when we laugh at it, the body releases endorphins for self-anaesthesia. This gives you that warm, tingling feeling after you laugh. Crying is often the extension of laughing. That is why in a serious emotional crisis, such as a death, many people cry but a person who cannot mentally accept the death may begin laughing. When the reality hits, however, the laughter then turns to crying. The bottom line is that laughter anaesthetises – calms – the body and builds the immune system to protect you against illness and disease. It's also been proven that laughter improves your health and extends your life. Telling jokes is good for you.

'Laughter releases tension and "psychic energy" that is beneficial for your health and that is why laughter is a coping mechanism for when you are upset, angry or sad.'
Sigmund Freud

Studies show that two minutes of laughing can lower blood pressure, reduce stress hormones and increase muscle flexion. It also boosts the immune function by raising levels of infection-fighting T-cells called interferon gamma and B-cells, which produce disease-destroying antibodies.

Most of us have experienced the physical effects that depression, mental strain or stress can have on our bodies, or the euphoria of a really good day that makes every ache or pain go away. We know that sleep can have an impact on our minds and emotions as well as our physical energy levels. Our emotions are fundamentally connected with all aspects of our health. Laughter exercises the internal organs, increases oxygen to the brain, boosts endorphins, strengthens the immune system, and brightens our moods and outlook on life.

The links between mental, emotional and physical health exploded when Louise Hay brought the concept into the public eye with her books *You Can Heal Your Body* and *You Can Heal Your Life*. These books became the benchmark for taking an holistic approach to healing. Our health, illnesses, and even the shape of our body have been linked to mental and emotional patterns that, over time, have implications for our physical reality.

Links between thought and cancer leaped ahead in 1971 when researchers Arthur Schmale and Howard Iker conducted a study that linked cancer of the cervix to the emotion of hopelessness. In 1977, Dr Keith Pettigale reported decreased serum IgA levels in patients who habitually suppressed anger. Serum IgA is linked to increased rates of metastatic breast cancer. In 1978, D.P. Spence, H.S. Scarborough and E.H. Ginsburg completed a study linking emotional factors to cervical cancer. Associate Professor Roger Bartro, from the University of New South Wales, found decreased T-cell functions in people during bereavement.

Dr Shevach Friedler, a physician who works in IVF and is also a graduate of the Jacques Lecoq School of Mime and Theatre in Paris, created a unique experiment that combined his background in clowning, movement and IVF. In a one-year experiment, he and his team at the Assaf Harofeh Medical Center in Zrifin, Israel, studied 219 women during a 'medical clowning encounter' after they had just undergone IVF. Half the women were treated to regular routines of tricks, jokes, magic and comedy, while the other half were not. Results showed that 36 per cent of women who were treated to a 20-minute comedy routine after in vitro fertilisation became pregnant. In contrast, only 20 per cent of women in the comedy-deprived group became pregnant.

For women wanting to get pregnant through IVF, the study demonstrates that humour is beneficial at the crucial moments after embryo transfer and may increase the chance of conception. Comedy acts as a de-stressor during what is, to many patients, a stressful medical procedure. The study also shows how humour is beneficial for women at the crucial moments after embryo transfer.

Medical clowns have been involved with paediatric and cancer care for some time, and their work with adult patients is rapidly growing.

**Life is too short to be serious all the time.
So, if you can't laugh at yourself, call me...
I'll laugh at you.**

How humour relieves stress

The American Medical Association (AMA) now estimates that over 80 per cent of all illnesses that cause a person to visit a doctor are stress related. Stress has been shown to be the main trigger for at least 85 per cent of all cancers and major diseases.

Stress is the trigger, however, not the cause. Laughter and humour have now been shown to be one of the most effective, chemical-free, cost-effective ways of dealing with 21st-century stress. Without laughter and a humorous perspective on things, you dramatically increase your odds of illness, early ageing, personal failures and premature death.

Everyone's life is full of stresses that deplete the immune system. The human body evolved to be able to deal with bursts of stress as they occurred. If ancestral man was chased by a sabre-toothed cat his body would experience a huge amount of stress, but only for a short time. If he fought enemies, the stress might last for up to an hour until the fight was over. If he didn't like his neighbours, he could remove the stress they caused by killing them quickly and then getting on with life. The human body is designed to deal with stress quickly, and then return to normal. For today's humans, however, the stress of 21st-century living is entirely different and something our bodies are not designed to cope with. The anxiety of having a large mortgage, the threat of being fired, getting divorced, serious illness, or financial problems can last for decades. We are not designed to cope with these events and the prolonged state of stress they often create.

The C3H mice

The crippling effects of stress were demonstrated by Vernon Riley at the University of Washington in Seattle in a pioneering experiment using C3H mice. These mice are bred for cancer research because, at a certain age, most will develop breast cancer. Riley found that by varying stress factors applied to the mice, he could vary the incidence of cancer from 7 per cent in low-stressed mice to 90 per cent in highly stressed mice. He showed how chronic stress increased steroid production and that a mouse tumor virus is more carcinogenic in the presence of elevated steroid levels. In humans, chronic stress levels have been shown as bad prognostic indicators in breast and lung cancer because of increased steroid production and the immune system being inhibited. Australian cancer authority Professor Philip Stricker OA told us that, after a cancer diagnosis, his patients can almost always pinpoint a major stressful event in their life in the past two to three years – usually events such as separation, divorce, bereavement, redundancy, accident, bankruptcy or serious financial problems.

Sydney oncologist Dr Joan Dale told us that the first question she asks her newly diagnosed cancer patients is, 'Do you own your own business or are you a corporate executive?' She found that if you are a high-flyer and under constant stress, you're a candidate for a major illness.

Research everywhere now concludes that chronic stress or a major stressful event is the trigger that can cause the onset of cancer and other major diseases. We all need some stress in our lives to keep us on the ball and moving forward, but human bodies are not designed to deal with chronic periods of stress. In other words, if you promote a C3H mouse to a senior executive position, give it a huge mortgage, put it into business for itself or send it to the divorce court or bankrupt it, its odds of dying from a major illness go through the roof.

Holding on to anger is like drinking poison and expecting the other person to die.

Laughing your way to health

Norman Cousins was a pioneer in laughter therapy and a catalyst for Patch Adams' research (see p. 175). Cousins was diagnosed with a terminal illness called ankylosing spondylitis, a degenerative disease that causes the breakdown of collagen, the fibrous tissue that binds together the body's cells. After becoming almost completely paralysed and given only a few months to live, Cousins checked out of the hospital and moved into a hotel room. Then he hired all the funny movies he could find. These included original *Candid Camera* tapes, old prints of Marx Brothers and Three Stooges movies, and every type of humorous show from sitcoms to satire and over-the-top comedies. On his first night in the hotel, Cousins reported that he laughed so hard at the films that he was able to stimulate chemicals in his body that allowed him several hours of pain-free sleep. When the pain returned he would simply watch another funny movie and the laughter would let him sleep again. He recorded the changes in his body by measuring his blood sedimentation rate, a key measurement of inflammation and infection in the blood. Cousins found that this rate dropped by at least five points each time he watched one of these films.

He watched them over and over, laughing as hard and loud as he could. After six months of this self-designed laughter therapy, the doctors were amazed to find that his illness had been completely cured – the disease had gone! This result led to Cousins publishing the book *Anatomy of an Illness*, which initiated the massive research into the function of the body chemical, endorphin. As we previously mentioned, endorphins are released by the brain when you laugh. They have a similar composition to morphine and heroin. Cousins' case demonstrated how laughter has a tranquillising effect on the body and builds the immune system, protecting you from disease. Cousins found that ten minutes of hard laughing gave him two hours of drug-free pain relief. The experiences he writes about in his book provided the medical breakthrough in explaining why happy people rarely get sick and why unhappy, miserable people always seem to be ill.

Norman Cousins' study and subsequent research reveals that ten minutes of hard laughing can give two hours of drug-free pain relief.

In December 1980, Cousins suffered a near-fatal heart attack while teaching in California. As he had done before, he made his body a personal laboratory. He refused morphine and made sure he had lots of rest and laughter. Gradually his condition improved. Cousins published his findings in another book titled *The Healing Heart*.

By the time of his death in 1990, Norman Cousins had received hundreds of awards including the Peace Medal from the United Nations and 49 honorary doctorates for having challenged the odds using non-traditional methods. Laughter works. And he who laughs last…

Take the Stress Test now

All major events in our lives produce some stress, and it is your ability or inability to adapt to these changes that makes the difference between getting ill or staying well. Psychiatrists Thomas Holmes and Richard Rahe decided to study whether or not stress contributes to illness. They surveyed more than 5,000 patients and asked them to say whether they had experienced any of a series of 44 life events in the previous two years. Below is a chart they created called the Social Readjustment Rating Scale, which shows the relative stress associated with various events in life.

This test can help show you if you're at risk of illness due to stress. Take it now and see how you score.

Event	Point Value
Death of spouse or partner	100
Threat of death	100
Divorce	73
Separation	65
Jail term	63
Death of close family member	63
Personal injury or illness	53
Marriage	50
Fired from work	47
Marital reconciliation	45
Retirement	45
Change in family member's health	44
Pregnancy	40
Sex difficulties	39
Addition to family	39
Business readjustment	39
Change in financial status	38
Death of close friend	37
Change to different line of work	36
Change in number of marital arguments	36
Large mortgage or loan (way above national average)	31
Foreclosure of mortgage or loan	30

Change in work responsibilities 29
Son or daughter leaving home 29
Trouble with in-laws 29
Outstanding personal achievement 28
Spouse begins or stops work 26
Starting or finishing school 26
Change in living conditions 25
Revision of personal habits 24
Trouble with boss 23
Change in work hours, conditions 20
Change in residence 20
Change in schools 20
Change in recreational habits 19
Change in church activities 19
Change in social activities 18
Mortgage or loan around the national average 17
Change in sleeping habits 16
Change in number of family gatherings 15
Change in eating habits 15
Vacation 13
Christmas season 12
Minor violation of the law 11

Your Score = _____

Scoring for your chances of becoming ill in the near future

11–150   Low to moderate
150–299   Moderate to high
300–600   High to very high chance of becoming ill in the near future.

You will notice that positive events such as marriage or retirement produce more stress than negative events such as being fired or the death of a close friend.

Holmes and Rahe found that a score of 300 in any one year produces a 50 per cent chance of developing an illness within one year. They also found that a score of under 200 produces a risk of less than 10 per cent.

Candace Pert's peptide research

Everyone has the ability to increase the temperature in their hands by 5 to 10 degrees Fahrenheit when they are connected to monitoring machines. This process of influencing your body's functioning while looking at a monitoring machine is called biofeedback. And it's done purely by using your thoughts.

In her book *Molecules of Emotion: Why You Feel the Way You Feel*, Candace Pert showed how emotions take the form of real, concrete substances in our body, called peptides. She found that the peptide (endorphin) produced by laughter flows through the body and has a direct, positive effect on body systems, including the immune system. This explains how our health is affected by emotions. These peptides are, medically speaking, the physical evidence of our emotions and they continually come into contact with our immune system, endocrine system and nervous system.

Depending on our emotional state (happy, sad, angry, etc.), different peptides are released and therefore different messages are sent throughout the body. For example, feelings of bliss and bonding are accompanied by the release of endorphins into the body's communication highway. Feelings of self-love are accompanied by a peptide called VIP (Vasoactive Intestinal Peptide). Each peptide has its own emotional tone or mood that you can experience.

As your emotions change, different peptides are released and send different messages throughout your body.

When we are stressed, we are focused on a problem and may be experiencing uncomfortable feelings and a lack of self-esteem. Laughter can release different chemicals into the peptide pool. This changes the peptide flow and can trigger more positive associations, memories, sense of self and feelings toward others. As a result, we are given a new outlook on life and the stressful situation. This is why it is so important to choose to think positive and humorous thoughts.

Learning to see the funny side of negative events has proven to be a powerful strategy in reducing stress, keeping illness at bay, increasing your success rate and extending life. Deciding to see the funny side is a choice that can be programmed through the RAS.

The Laughter Room

In the 1980s several American hospitals introduced the concept of the 'Laughter Room', based on Norman Cousins' experiences. This room was filled with joke books, comedy films and other humorous material, and comedians or clowns would often visit. The results have shown an improvement in patients' health and immune systems, and shorter average hospitalisation times. After laughing, a patient's pulse rate steadies, breathing deepens and the muscles relax. This all helps a patient to get through an illness. In addition to shorter hospital stays for many patients, participating hospitals have also recorded a decrease in the number of painkillers required and report that patients are easier to deal with.

So you need to take your laughter seriously. Most people take themselves too seriously. They see themselves as very important in the overall scheme of things in life – important to the community, vital to a relationship and indispensable at work. Unfortunately, the result of the stress associated with this self-importance includes ulcers, haemorrhoids, high blood pressure, heart conditions and other major illnesses.

To demonstrate how much everyone will miss you if you leave your job, neighbourhood or social group, take a bucket and fill it with water. Put your arm in the water up to your elbow and then pull it out as quickly as you can. Now look into the bucket. The hole that is left in the water is the hole that you'll leave when you're gone.

A TRUE STORY – HUNTER CAMPBELL

After experiencing many distressing situations in his life, including the death of several loved ones, Hunter Campbell suffered from depression, contemplated suicide and ended up in a psychiatric hospital. After he was discharged from hospital, he enrolled in medical school.

While in medical school, he visited patients and enjoyed performing funny tricks and making his patients laugh. At the same time, he observed how many patients experienced a dramatic improvement in their health when they laughed regularly. Campbell finished medical school and became a doctor under his new nickname, Patch Adams. Throughout his career he continued to use laughter and fun with his patients as a form of therapy.

In addition to using the effects of laughter in his practice, he also founded a hospital, the Gesundheit Institute, where the doctors work for little money and the patients are never billed for services. Since the

1980s, Adams has brought his unique brand of laughter therapy to more than 50 countries, including war-torn nations such as Bosnia and Afghanistan. Every year Adams takes a troupe of volunteer clowns to Russia where they bring hope and fun to hospitals, orphanages and care homes for the elderly. Dressed in loud, colourful clothing, with long blue hair tied back in a ponytail, Adams – along with a brigade of volunteers and a giant inflatable chicken – regularly clowns for groups of young cancer patients there. Doctors at the Paediatric Oncology Institute in Moscow say that visits from clowns have a tangible effect on the health of patients. Dr Yevgenia Moiseyenko reported that Patch Adams' therapies gave children the strength to fight their illness and that their health improved noticeably.

Patch Adams was the first doctor to formally recognise that a happy person has a stronger immune system and is much less susceptible to illness and disease and the symptoms of stress than an unhappy person. His findings were captured in the award-winning movie Patch Adams starring Robin Williams.

'Innumerable studies have now demonstrated the link between humour, laughter, good mood and recovery from illness . . . People who don't laugh often or are usually in a bad mood may be what psychologist Eysenck called "the disease-prone personality" – more likely to get sick and less likely to heal than their more optimistic peers or other patients with the same diagnosis. The reverse is also true . . . A person's attitude about his disease can affect his chances of healing and the rate at which his health improves.'
Patch Adams

Choosing your emotions

Several emotions such as anger, jealousy and remorse serve useful purposes for human survival. Jealousy, for example, appears to be a hardwired emotion to keep competitors away from our mates, and remorse builds close bonds with others in regrettable circumstances. But there are four emotions that are destructive and counter-productive to your happiness – guilt, embarrassment, shame and offence.

Babies don't feel guilty, embarrassed, offended or ashamed. These are all emotions we learn as adults. Embarrassment means that you give more power to the opinions others hold of you than to your opinion of yourself. For example, you get locked out of your home in your underwear and the neighbours see you. You only feel embarrassed if their opinion of why you are outdoors in your underwear – they think you're kinky, perhaps – is more important than your own opinion of the truth about what really happened.

It's only when what others think about you is more important than your own opinion that you can feel embarrassed. In a similar way, guilt and shame can only exist when you allow yourself to be judged by the opinions, expectations or rules of others. Guilt and shame are two of the main emotions used in religion to control followers by dictating their choices and responses to events. Break a law and you will be shamed into doing what the leaders or the figureheads demand.

Guilt, embarrassment, shame and offence are emotions that are learned and are detrimental to your success in life.

Being offended is also a choice. Others can't offend you – you can only choose to feel offended. Offence is not something someone does to you; it's an attitude you take. Choosing offence tells the world that you are unable to come to terms with the problems in your life. Calm and successful people choose not to take offence – they hold the position that what anyone else may think is their opinion, and that's all.

These four emotions are all choices, and it doesn't make sense for you to choose them as they are more harmful to your success than useful. Choosing any of these four attitudes shows others that either you aren't in control of your own emotions or you are likely to have low self-esteem.

There are also people with certain medical conditions who don't feel these four negative emotions. These include those with ADHD, autism and Asperger's Syndrome. As a result, they have difficulty reading human emotions and are unaware of how another person might be feeling, but this is due to their particular affliction, not by their choice. These people are also unable to read body language signals, which are the main key to someone's feelings and are consequently often seen by others as uncaring and insensitive.

Develop a humour repertoire for your circumstances

Think about how you can develop a humorous repertoire for any stressful circumstances life serves up. There are almost no circumstances that don't have a humorous side, including death. You just need to look for it.

Barb and I lived in England for 11 years and the locals would regularly tell Australian jokes about us. For example:

'*What's the difference between Australia and yoghurt? Yoghurt has some culture!*'

'*Aussies are well balanced. They have a chip on both shoulders.*'

'*Aussies are level-headed. They drool from both sides of their mouth.*'

'*You can tell an Australian – but you can't tell him much!*'

'*Aussies wear shorts to get air to the brain.*'

We could easily have chosen to be offended by these quips but we decided to see the funny side instead, and laughed with the locals. Being offended – or not – is always a choice.

When I was receiving treatment for prostate cancer, I created a series of humorous lines to deal with the stress of having strange men sticking their fingers where the sun doesn't shine. I gave these lines to other prostate cancer patients and most had a fun time using them. These lines included:

'*Does this mean we're engaged, Doc? We must be because you've got my ring on your finger!*'

'*This is like the* Starship Enterprise, *Doc. You're boldly going where no man has gone before!*'

'*Can you hear me NOW, Doc?*'

'*You know, Doc, in New Zealand, we're legally married now!*'

'*So this is how Kermit the Frog feels!*'

'*Hey, Doc, could you write a note to my wife and tell her that my head is **not** up there?*'

These lines made everyone laugh, released endorphins into the blood, entertained the doctors and helped us deal with uncomfortable circumstances.

Summary

There's always a funny side to any negative event that happens in life. You just have to choose to look for it. And the more serious the event, the funnier you can make it.

You can choose to be angry because the traffic is at a standstill. But it won't clear the traffic – it will just raise your stress levels. If you choose – through your RAS – to take a calm, analytical approach to the problem of the traffic jam, you may come up with an answer that can help you feel better.

Having a sense of humour and laughing about life have been proven to significantly improve your health, help you to de-stress, build relationships with others and reach higher success levels.

Norman Cousins' story led to many new ways of thinking that helped contribute to the rise of laughter clubs, comedy stores and hospital laughter rooms. Ultimately, laughter represents the enthusiasm of the human spirit, and in this we can find our way back to good health.

We hold the power to use our conscious mind to change our physical state of being. In understanding humour, we use our conscious mind, but at the same time, thanks to the RAS, our actual physical response to humour and laughter changes certain elements in our body in a way that is beneficial to our health.

Like most natural remedies, laughter is not an absolute cure. But it has proven to be a powerful medical tool in a surprising number of health situations and is helpful in decreasing pain and easing tension. So next time you're at home sick with a cold, forget the chicken soup and cough syrup – take a day off and try some classic laughter therapy with your favourite comedies. Taking yourself too seriously is detrimental to your health.

**To give yourself a reality check,
always remember that the size of your
funeral will depend on the weather.**

Decide now to choose to look mainly at the funny side of everything that happens in life, especially the negative things. You can choose to feel offended because someone tells a joke that says people in your occupation or from your country are stupid. That doesn't mean that they are stupid, and even if you agree that maybe they are, abusing the joke-teller won't make them any smarter.

You can feel upset because it rains on your birthday party, but the rain doesn't care – it just keeps raining.

Make the decision never again to choose the emotions of guilt, shame, embarrassment or offence, and never to become angry about things that are unchangeable.

**Holding a grudge is like letting someone
live rent-free in your head.**

Take what you do in life seriously. But never take yourself too seriously. It's bad for your health and others won't invite you around for dinner.

**Always laugh when you can.
It's cheaper than medicine.**

Chapter 12

Overcoming Fear and Worry

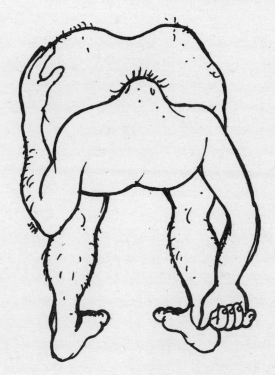

**John's way of dealing with life's problems
never seemed to get results.**

*One day a farmer's donkey fell into a well. The animal cried for hours as
the farmer tried to figure out what to do. Finally, he decided the animal
was old, and the well needed to be covered up anyway; it just wasn't
worth trying to retrieve the donkey. He invited all his neighbours to come
over and help him. They each grabbed a shovel and began to shovel dirt*

into the well. At first, the donkey realised what was happening and cried in fear. Then he suddenly went silent.

A few shovel loads later, the farmer looked down the well. He was stunned by what he saw. With each shovel of dirt that hit his back, the donkey was doing something amazing. He would shake it off and take a step up. As the farmer's neighbours continued to shovel dirt on top of the animal, he would shake it off and take a step up. Soon, everyone was amazed as the donkey stepped up over the edge of the well and trotted off!

The Moral: *Life is going to shovel all kinds of dirt on you whether you like it or not. The trick to getting out of a hole is to shake off the dirt and take a step up. Each of your troubles is, in fact, a stepping stone to getting out. We can climb out of the deepest wells by not stopping and never giving up! Shake it off and take a step up.*

Next day, the donkey came back and kicked the crap out of the people who tried to bury him. Always remember that if you think that covering your ass is the easy way out, it will always come back to bite you.

The two greatest obstacles to achieving success, happiness, fulfilment and inner peace are fear and worry. These two responses are linked to our 'fight or flight' response, which comes from our ancient past and evolved to reduce our chances of death. These emotions come in various forms that have been shown to harm many of the organs of the body. Anger has been shown to weaken the liver, worry weakens the stomach, stress weakens the heart, grief weakens the lungs, and fear weakens the kidneys.

Fear is nothing more than a physical reaction to thinking about the consequences you don't want. This creates an electrical energy in the brain that transfers to the physical body.

Importantly, all forms of fear are stress-related and deplete the immune system. This is why people who live fearful lives are constantly sick and suffer a range of debilitating illnesses.

The key to creating a successful life is to learn how to develop a winning mindset, and to control worry and fear rather than letting them control you.

Worrying is like praying for what you don't want.

The science behind fear

The emotions of fear and worry come from your central nervous system. They are memories that are stored in specific regions of the brain and can be triggered by any number of stimuli in your daily life. We often think of memories as our experiences or impressions, facts or details that we can recall at will. But neuroscientists have found that we have several different types of memory, and each one traces a separate neural pathway in the brain.

Dr Elizabeth Phelps, Professor of Psychology and Neural Science at New York University, has devoted her career to discovering how these neural systems work. She uses cognitive neuroscience to investigate the relationship between emotion and memory. Dr Phelps has found that there are two basic types of memory – explicit memory and implicit memory. The first – explicit memory – is when you remember facts, details and impressions. It's the memory that activates when you read a menu and your mouth begins to salivate, or you hear a song from your past that affects you emotionally or can even make you cry. The brain's hippocampus handles the storage and retrieval of explicit memories, and these are the ones we can choose to remember.

The second is implicit memory, which is learned. Stored

reactions from past emotional events and experiences are linked to the automatic physical responses. The brain's threat centre – the amygdala – stores implicit memories on a subconscious level. For example, fear is an implicit memory because it allows us to react quickly for survival if necessary.

Scientists now believe that humans evolved with this process in the brain to allow us to respond quickly to a dangerous situation without having to think about it. For example, the fear of a loud sound lets you respond quickly to a potentially dangerous event. Professor Joseph LeDoux of New York University describes two pathways of differing lengths that fear signals follow within the brain. His experiments show that our sensory organs pass information to the thalamus, where signals split and trace two separate paths on their way to the brain's threat centre, the amygdala.

Following the shorter path, one signal sounds the fear alarm before we're even aware of the situation. The other reaches the sensory cortex a fraction of a second later, providing a much clearer picture of the potential threat. The second signal can reinforce the fear response or declare a false alarm.

For example, a person runs up to you on the street and mugs you. Next time you see someone running toward you, the fear response is likely to be triggered again, in anticipation. The fear response has been learned by a process called classical conditioning, mediated by the amygdala.

Early fear experiments

How these two different memories work was first documented in 1911 when the Swiss psychologist Édouard Claparède conducted an experiment with a patient who had suffered brain damage and seemed unable to form new memories.

Every time Claparède interviewed the patient, she had no recollection of having ever seen him before. So each time they met he would reintroduce himself and shake the patient's hand. Then he had an idea: he held out his hand to greet her, but this time he had concealed a tack in his hand. Naturally, she pulled her hand away when pricked by the tack. The next time they met, although she still failed to recognise him, the patient refused to shake his hand, but could not say why. Claparède's experiment with his patient showed that the avoidance response of fear can be learned without consciousness. This explains why we can feel fearful without knowing why.

Sometimes, certain memories are stored in both the explicit and implicit memory banks. For example, when you visit the dentist, your implicit memory reacts to the smell of antiseptic before you are consciously aware of it. This can trigger your explicit memory to retrieve the vision of a needle. When you hear the sound of the dentist's drill, your explicit memory can go into overdrive.

'Life is like a roller coaster. You can either scream at every bump or you can throw your hands in the air and go for the ride.'
Anonymous

Stress hormones released by the fear system strengthen memory pathways in our brains, allowing us to easily recall memories of emotional experiences. These are called 'flash-bulb memories'. For example, most Baby Boomers easily recall what they were doing when they heard that John F. Kennedy had been shot, and most of Generation X can recall where they were when they heard that Princess Diana had been killed. Researchers have also found that if an emotional event becomes too traumatic, it can negatively affect memory. Even though people report vivid recollections related to flash-bulb memories, they will often swear by details that are in fact wrong.

Why fear is important to us

In evolutionary terms, 'fearless' animals would have been less likely to survive because they would not retreat from dangerous situations. This is also why, in humans, fear is an important response. For humans in the 21st century, however, these fears can show themselves as shyness, loss of self-confidence, anxiety disorders, fear of failure and fear to move ahead from where we are now.

Despite the primary function of fear – to help us get out of dangerous, physically threatening situations – many popular pastimes are fuelled by our attraction to it. For example, watching scary movies, bungee-jumping, visiting horror houses, playing extreme sports and riding roller coasters. Thrill-seeking daredevils get enjoyment out of these fear-inducing activities because their levels of the neurotransmitter dopamine increase dramatically during them. They experience feelings of pleasure or euphoria – similar to the feelings drug addicts get.

Our brains are unable to distinguish between truly

frightening experiences and those that are intentionally designed to frighten us. That's how scary activities allow us to experience fear without actually exposing us to real physical danger. When you watch a scary movie, for example, your fear hormones dramatically increase, giving something akin to a drug hit.

In our opinion, the top five scariest movies ever made are:

1. *The Exorcist*
2. *The Shining*
3. *Psycho*
4. *The Silence of the Lambs*
5. *Jaws*

Fear can be positive or negative

Reasonable fear is good for your safety, but it can also become disabling in anxiety disorders such as Post-Traumatic Stress Disorder, Panic Disorder, Social Anxiety Disorder or Obsessive Compulsive Disorder. Anxiety disorders reflect runaway activity in the parts of the brain that control fear.

These disorders cause emotional and physical symptoms that can be annoying or crippling, and they affect people of all ages and both sexes. For example, each year in the United States more than 40 million Americans – about 18 per cent of the adult population – suffer from some form of anxiety disorder.

'The cave you most fear to enter contains the greatest treasure.'
Brian Tracy

The most common fears are social ones: the fear of situations in which others are likely to judge you. For example, the fear of public speaking seriously affects around 50 per cent of people. Most people get butterflies in the stomach before speaking to a group, and millions of people feel intimidated just walking into a room full of strangers.

Public speaking has been shown to be number one on the list of most people's fears.
Fear of death sits, on average, at number seven.
Does this mean that, at a funeral, it's better to be in the coffin than reading the eulogy?

Although stepping up to a podium may not seem like being chased by a hungry lion, it releases the same responses in our bodies. Scientists believe our social fears are related to our concern for survival because groups help us stay alive and we fear situations that could lead to our exclusion from a group.

The positive side of fear

Chronic fear and anxiety sap your resources, causing your self-healing and preserving mechanisms to be inefficient. The longer you experience these emotions, the worse your overall health becomes. Your current memories are deeply established electrical and chemical connections that exist between the billions of interactive surfaces in the nerve cells that make up your brain. The triggers for chronic fear and anxiety do not present acute danger to your life. To overcome these false fear and anxiety responses, you need to create new memories that can modify your central nervous system.

The solution: if you catch yourself thinking about the outcomes you don't want, choose to change that picture and only think about the outcomes you do want. It's that simple.

Fear of rejection

The first thing to understand about rejection is that it will happen to you constantly when you are moving forward. Any person who has ever achieved any significant level of success has learned to deal with the rejections that happen along the way. We all get rejected regularly – you asked someone to marry you and they said 'No', your request for a pay rise was refused, your application to university was rejected, a client wouldn't buy from you, someone cancelled their appointment with you, or maybe no-one liked your great idea.

But a rejection doesn't mean your situation becomes worse. For example, if you applied to join the police force and they said no because you didn't measure up to some requirement, you haven't lost anything – you weren't in the police force before you applied and you're still not in it after your rejection. If you ask someone to go on a date with you and the say 'No', nothing has changed. You still don't have a date with that person. If you submit a design to your bosses and they reject it, you are still no worse off than before you submitted the design. In fact you are better off after a rejection because you now know what to do to modify your idea or approach in order to have a better shot at it next time.

**'Most people achieved their greatest
success one step beyond what looked
like their greatest failure.'
Brian Tracy**

Scientific evidence indicates that our responses to rejection could be hardwired into our brain because, in ancient times, being rejected from your tribe usually reduced your odds for survival. This is why most people experience panic and fear when they are rejected by a group, a lover or even rejected in a job application. Even though the situation is not as serious as it would have been in ancestral times – you can always stand a good chance of getting another job, a new partner or social group – the brain and body can react as if the situation were life-threatening.

If you think back to a time when you experienced physical pain, such as a burn or twisted ankle, you can recall being in pain but you don't actually feel the pain again as you remember it. When you recall a rejection, however, you can relive that pain as if it were happening to you right now. The memory of the rejection is more powerful than the memory of physical pain. To deal with this response, our brains have a built-in coping mechanism that releases 'opioids' after we experience a rejection. This is exactly the same mechanism that kicks in when we experience physical pain. Opioids give us a quick fix – a 'high' to counteract the 'low' of the rejection. Side effects of this response include a temporarily lower IQ, which affects our decision-making ability and increases aggression levels.

These are also the main drivers behind situations such as extreme physical attacks on a partner or school shootings.

When you are on the receiving end of a rejection, here's a simple way to handle it:

1. Don't take it personally
Understand that you are hardwired to experience emotional pain and it's difficult to avoid feeling bad.

2. Give yourself permission to feel bad
When you are rejected allow yourself to experience the feelings.

3. Put a time limit on it
Make a conscious decision to stop thinking about the rejection by a specific time. For example, decide that by eight o'clock tonight or midday tomorrow you'll stop thinking about it. After that time you will choose only to think about what you do want to happen or what you can do. In other words, move on. If you don't set a time limit, you can sink into long-term depression and end up on Prozac – or worse.

If you are going to deliver a rejection to another person, here's a painless but effective way to do it:

1. Thank them
'Thank you for applying for this position.'
'Thank you for asking me out on a date.'
'Thank you for submitting your ideas.'

2. Explain why you have rejected them
'We need a candidate who has more experience/skills/can travel.'
'I'm in a complicated relationship right now, so I can't accept your dinner invitation.'
'We need to study a wide range of ideas first.'

3. Praise their positives
'*You have many excellent skills/attributes/qualities that should land you a suitable role.*'
'*There are many women/men here who would love to say "Yes" to you.*'
'*There are businesses which would jump at your ideas.*'

Three simple ways to deal with fear

1. Take time out
If you are feeling threatened or intimidated by a situation, the first thing to do is take time out so you can physically calm down. A racing heart, sweating palms and feeling helpless and confused are the result of adrenalin. Take at least 15 minutes off and go for a walk, take a shower or make a cup of tea or coffee. You can't think clearly when you're full of fear or anxiety.

2. Be realistic
Many people affirm to themselves that they are going to fail at something because they failed at something else in their past. But their fears are usually worse than the reality. For example, people who have been at a beach when a shark is spotted start to imagine sharks at every beach they visit. People who have been physically attacked start thinking they're going to be attacked again when they walk into a dark street. Remind yourself of the times when you have overcome obstacles in the past. You've done it before, and you can do it again.

3. Go back to basics
Many people use drugs or alcohol to self-treat their anxiety, hoping it will make them feel better, but these things only

make fears worse. A good sleep, an enjoyable meal or a walk are often the best cures for anxiety or tension.

Here are some other good alternatives:
- Eat well; you will feel great physically and mentally.
- Read, watch or listen to something inspirational.
- Call a friend who has the ability to talk you through things and who can make you feel good.
- Youtube.com is full of inspirational stories that you can access immediately for free.
- Watch motivational presentations by Anthony Robbins, Brian Tracy and Allan Pease.

Summary

Fear is an integral and important element in the human brain. Feeling fearful or concerned about your life is normal human behaviour. Fearless animals in any species usually don't live long and fearless species become extinct.

Worry and fear often result from feelings of inadequacy when we compare ourselves to other people who we think are better than us. The only time it's healthy to compare yourself to another person is when someone is ahead of you and you use them as a source of inspiration.

Courage is the mastery of fear, not the avoidance of it. Courage means feeling the fear and taking action anyway.

Many people live every day with the memories of their failures – marriage, bankruptcy, getting fired or losing something important. They continually relive these events, they bore everyone senseless talking about them and don't notice that others have stopped inviting them to social functions.

When something is over, decide that it's over – put a deadline on when you will stop talking about it or thinking about it. It's not easy, but it's that simple. And you don't need drugs. Positive thoughts create an abundance of the feel-good hormones such as serotonin and dopamine, which pharmaceutical drugs try to replace.

Remember that sometimes the bad things that happen in our lives put us directly on the path to the best things that will ever happen to us.

Of all the things we worry about in life, studies have shown that most things won't happen and you have little or no control over the few things that do happen. Here's what has been found about our problems:

87 per cent never happen
7 per cent actually occur
6 per cent you will have some influence over

So it doesn't pay to worry about the things you fear. Most of your worries will never eventuate and most fears are nothing more than:

False Evidence Appearing Real.

Finally, ask yourself this question: *What's the worst that can happen?*

When you're anxious or fearful about something, think about what the worst result could be. Whether it's a presentation, a phone call, a conversation or a relationship that goes horribly wrong, the sun will still come up the next morning and life will continue. To put your own fears into perspective, find a way to help someone in need or who is less fortunate than you. You will realise how lucky you are and your problems will look less daunting.

**'If you are depressed you are living in the past.
If you are anxious you are living in the future.
If you are at peace you are living in the present.'
Lao Tzu**

Fear has two meanings:

Forget Everything and Run
Face Everything and Rise.

The choice is yours.

Fear does not prevent death. It prevents life.

Chapter 13

Never Give Up

LEAP OF FAITH

WHERE YOU ARE NOW

WHERE YOU WANT TO BE

MAKE THE JUMP!

**Winners are not people who never fail,
but people who never quit.**

Every person who ever succeeded at anything faced tons of rejection. This includes few or no results, little money, no promotion, pain, criticism, poor evaluation, unhappiness, complaints and loneliness. Rejection is, however, a critical sign to show you where you need to improve and what you need to do to get more praise, happiness, money, promotions and better results. As mentioned, rejection is nothing more than negative feedback that is showing you what *not* to do. In fact, the negative feedback you receive from rejection is so important that you should welcome it because it shows you the right path to the success you want. History is filled with examples of people who held fast to their vision and used negative feedback to move forward.

Walt Disney was fired from a newspaper for *'lacking imagination and having no original ideas'*. Disney's theme park concept received over 300 rejections by banks, councils, financiers and local authorities before he finally created Disneyland. At age 30, Steve Jobs was brutally dumped by the board of Apple Computers, the company he had founded. Oprah Winfrey was demoted from her job as a news anchor because she *'wasn't fit for television'*, and the Beatles were rejected by Decca Studios because *'We don't like their sound. They have no future in show business.'* Even Albert Einstein's school report said he would *'never amount to much'*.

Where these people differ from most others is that they chose to stick with their goals, despite what others said, thought or did.

If you give up, you'll never know what you'll be missing. If you have an idea or concept you believe in and which you think will benefit others, stick with it. Don't give up early. As you move toward your goals some people will throw rocks at you, but you can choose whether to use those rocks to build a wall or to build a bridge.

Ninety-seven per cent of the people who quit too soon are employed by the 3 per cent who never gave up.

Ask the experts

Seek out people who have already done what you are planning to achieve. Whether it's beating cancer, climbing Mount Everest, riding a horse, learning another language, accumulating wealth, losing weight or growing organic food, there are plenty of people who have already done it. Some have written books about it, many produce courses, videos and manuals on it and you will find most on YouTube. Look on the Internet to see who they are and where to find them. Try inviting an expert to lunch or coffee and ask them to guide or mentor you. If they reject your initial approach, ask again. If they still say 'No', ask again. That's how they got to be successful themselves. Every expert was once a beginner looking for someone to help them find the right direction.

They can show you the shortcuts and pitfalls on the way to your goal. Don't reinvent the wheel – ask the experts how they did it. Do not ask the advice or opinions of people who have never done what you want to do. They can only tell you why it can't be done.

When you were a kid, you asked for what you wanted over and over again until someone gave it to you. If the first person didn't give it to you, the next one might, and if not that person, maybe the next. Kids are experts at wearing down their parents so they eventually get what they want. Ask, ask and ask again for what you want. The person you are asking today usually feels differently on different days, so chances are you'll pick a day when they feel ready to say 'Yes'. Don't keep what you want a secret, and never wait around for someone to work it out or give it to you. It won't happen.

As simple as this may sound, asking for what you want can

lead to great results. Yet asking is one of the toughest things most people are prepared to consider. They would love a raise, a donation, a date, a better seat, an airline upgrade or for their child to change teachers at school, but they won't ask in case the answer is 'No'.

The golden rule for asking is to keep doing it. Stick with it. Ask people continually for what you want. We don't mean that you should nag them. We mean that you should keep asking the decision makers in positive, creative ways to give you what you want. Statistically speaking, the answer is more likely to be 'No' than 'Yes', but if the ratio is, say, 10:1, you will eventually get one 'Yes'.

Even when the answer is 'No', you are no worse off than before you asked. You are in exactly the same position.

When you ask, be absolutely clear about what you are asking for. If you are going to ask someone for a date, don't say, *'Maybe we should go out sometime…'* Instead say, *'I'd like to take you to dinner and then to the movies on Saturday night. What's a good time to pick you up? Seven o'clock, or would eight be better?'*

Approach others as if it's a done deal and that it's the logical thing to do. *'I'd like a pay rise of $600 a month'* is more likely to get a *'Yes'* than *'I need a raise.'*

'Obsessed' is a word lazy people often use to describe dedicated people.

Decide right now to ask others to help you with your goals. Ask for that raise, a date, a referral, an introduction, a loan, mentoring advice, or whatever you need to move forward with your goals. And never give up asking. Someone, somewhere is waiting to say 'Yes' to whatever ideas you have. You may need to ask another 10, perhaps 20, or maybe more than 100 people, but someone is definitely waiting for you. As you now know, it's a matter of statistics. Don't feel despondent or depressed if someone says 'No' – simply ask the next person.

A TRUE STORY – *BODY LANGUAGE*

When I completed the manuscript for the book Body Language *in 1978, I called on the major publishers in Australia but no-one wanted it or showed any interest. They had never heard of this concept, didn't know me, thought my manuscript was 'very American' and were generally dismissive of the idea. So I decided to publish it myself.*

I didn't know how to publish it but I had decided that I would do it, and that was the most important thing. After receiving my 35th rejection, a friend gave me a book on how to self-publish a book.

I needed $7,000 to publish it, so for the next six months I gave speeches on Body Language to any audience who'd listen, and I offered my upcoming book to attendees for $10 as an advance purchase and said I'd autograph it. Within six months I had raised $7,000 in pre-sales and published Body Language. *I then sourced a small distributor who would sell it into the bookstores on commission. I wrote a press release and sent it (under a friend's name) to all the major media, outlining to them that I was a humorous, entertaining and thought-provoking guest. Two days later I got a call from Australia's biggest TV talk show, The Mike Walsh Show. Their lead guest had just cancelled and 'Could I come in immediately as a replacement?' I showered, shaved, dressed and arrived at Channel 9 in record time! They gave me 18 minutes of airtime and within two weeks* Body Language *was number one in Australia.*

A river cuts through rock – not because of its power because of its persistence.

Armed with the Australian success of Body Language, I spent days gathering the addresses of US and UK publishers to give them the opportunity to publish my book. I wrote to the top 53 publishers, figuring that, statistically speaking, I'd have to get an offer somewhere.

Here's part of the actual list of publishers I contacted:

drey, R., *The Territorial Imperative*, Collins, London, 1967

gyle, M., *The Psychology of Interpersonal Behaviour*, Penguin Books, 1967

gyle, M., *Bodily Communication*, Methuen, London, 1975

gyle, M., *Skills with People: A Guide for Managers*, Hutchinson, London, 1973

gyle, M., *Training Managers*, The Acton Society Trust, London, 1962

gyle, M., *Social Interaction*, Methuen, London, 1968

on, A.M., *A Manual of Gestures*, Griggs, Chicago, 1875

thall, J. and Polhemus, T., *The Body as a Medium of Expression*, Allen Lane, London, 1975

ne, E., *Games People Play*, Grove Press, New York, 1964

whistell, R.L., *Introduction to Kinesics*, University of Louisville Press, Louisville, Kentucky, 1952

whistell, R.L., *Kinesics and Context*, Allen Lane, London, 1971

king, J., *Anthropology of the Body*, Academic Press, London, New York, 1977

an, W.J., *The Psychology of Jury Selection*, Vantage Press, New York, 1971

n, T., *The International Dictionary of Sign Language*, Wolfe Publishing, London, 1969

rn, H, *Winning the Negotiation*, Hawthorn Books, New York, 1979

Hess, E., *The Tell-Tale Eye*, Van Nostrand Reinhold, New York, 1975

Hind, R., *Non-Verbal Communication*, Cambridge University Press, London, 1972

Hore, T. *Non-Verbal Behaviour*, Australian Council for Educational Research, 1976

James, W., *Principles of Psychology*, Holt, Rinehart, New York, 1892

Jung, C., *Man and his Symbols*, Aldus, London, 1964

Kahn, R.L., and Cannell, C.F., *The Dynamics of Interviewing*, Wiley, New York, 1957

Kendon, A., *Organisation of Behaviour in Face-to-Face Interaction*, Mouton, The Hague, 1975

Carnegie, D., *How to Win Friends and Influence People*, Angus and Robertson, Sydney, 1965

Collett, P., *Social Rules and Social Behaviour*, Blackwell, Oxford, 1977

Critchley, M., *The Language of Gesture*, Arnold, London, 1939

Critchley, M., *Silent Language*, Butterworth, London, 1975

Cundiff, M., *Kinesics*, Parker Publishing, New York, 1972

Dale-Guthrie, R., *Body Hot-Spots*, Van Nostrand Reinhold, New York, 1976

Darwin, C., *The Expression of Emotion in Man and Animals*, Appleton-Century-Crofts, New York, 1872

Davitz, J.R., *The Communication of Emotional Meaning*, McGraw-Hill, New York, 1964

Duncan, S., and Fiske, D.W., *Face-to-Face Interaction*, Erlbaum, Hillsdale, New Jersey, 1977

Dunkell, S., *Sleep Positions*, Heinemann, London, 1977

Effron, D., *Gesture, Race and Culture*, Mouton, The Hague, 1972

Eibl-Eibesfeldt, I., *Ethology: The Biology of Behaviour*, Holt, Rinehart and Winston, New York, 1970

Eibl-Eibesfeldt, I., *Love and Hate: The Natural History of Behaviour Patterns*, Holt, Rinehart and Winston, New York, 1971

Ekman, P., *Darwin and Facial Expression*, Academic Press, New York, 1973

Mallery, G., *The Gesture Speech of M* Salem, 1881

Masters, W.H. and Johnson, V.E., *Human Sexual Response*, Little, Brown, Boston, 1966

Mehrabian, A., *Tactics in Social Influence*, Prentice-Hall, Englewood Cliffs, New Jersey, 1969

Mehrabian, A., *Silent Messages*, Wadsworth, Belmont, California, 1971

Mitchell, M.E., *How to Read the Language of the Face*, Macmillan, New York, 1968

Morris, D., *The Naked Ape*, Cape, London, 1967

Morris, D., *The Human Zoo*, Cape, London, 1969

Morris, D., *Intimate Behaviour*, Cape, London, 1971

Morris, D., *Manwatching*, Cape, London, 1977

Morris, D., with Collett, Marsh and O'Shaughnessy, *Gestures, their Origins and Distribution*, Cape, London, 1979

Nierenberg, G., *The Art of Negotiating*, Hawthorn Books, New York, 1968

Nierenberg, G., and Calero, H., *How to Read a Person like a Book*, Hawthorn Books, New York, 1971

Pease, A.V., *The Hot Button Selling System*, Elvic & Co, Sydney, 1976

Pliner, O., Kramer, L., Alloway, T., *Nonverbal Communication*, Plenum Press, New York, 1973

Reik, T., *Listening with the Third Ear*, Farrar, Straus and Giroux, New York, 1948

Saitz, R.L. and Cervenka, E.C., *Handbook of Gestures: Columbia and the United States*, Mouton, The Hague, 1972

Sathre, F., Olson, R., and Whitney, C., *Let's Talk*, Scott Foresman, Glenview, Illinois, 1973

Feldman, S., *Mannerisms of Speech and Gesture in Everyday Life*, International University Press, 1959

Gayle, W., *Power Selling*, Prentice-Hall, New York, 1959

Goffman, E., *Interaction Ritual*, Allen Lane, London, 1972

Goffman, E., *The Presentation of Self in Everyday Life*, Edinburgh University Press, Edinburgh, 1956

Goffman, E., *Behaviour in Public Places*, Free Press, Illinois, 1963

Gordon, R.L., *Interviewing Strategy, Techniques and Tactics*, Dorsey, Homewood, Illinois, 1976

Hall, E.T., *Silent Language*, Doubleday & Co., New York, 1959

Hall, E.T., *The Hidden Dimension*, Doubleday & Co., New York, 1966

Harper, R.G., *Non-Verbal Communication: the State of the Art*, Wiley, New York, 1978

Henley, N.M., *Body Politics: Power, Sex and Non-Verbal Communication*, Prentice-Hall, New Jersey, 1977

Scheflen, A.E., *Body Language Order*, Prentice-Hall, New

Scheflen, A.E., *Human Territory*, Hall, New Jersey, 1976

Schutz, W.C., *A Three-Dimensional Interpersonal Behaviour*, and Winston, New York,

Siddons, H., *Practical Illustrations of cal Gestures*, London, 18

Sommer, R., *Personal Space: al Basis of Design*, Prentice-wood Cliffs, New Jersey,

Szasz, S., *Body Language of Children*, New York, 1978

Whiteside, R.L., *Face Language*, Books, New York, 1975

Whitney, Hubin and Murphy, *Psychology of Persuasion in Selling*, Prentice-Hall, 1

Wolfe, C., *A Psychology of Gesture*, London, 1948

Von Cranach, M., *Social Communication and Movement: Studies of Expression in Man and Animals*, Academic Press, London,

Korda, M., *Power! How To Use It*, Weidenfeld & Nicolson, 1975

Korda, M., *Power in the Office*, & Nicolson, London, 1976

Korman, B., *Hands: The Power of Sunridge Press, New York,

Lamb, W., *Posture and Gesture*, London, 1965

Lamb, W., *Body Code*, Routledge & Paul, London, 1979

Lewis, D., *The Secret Language* Souvenir Press, London, 1

Liggett, J., *The Human Face*, London, 1974

Lorenz, K., *On Aggression*, Methuen, 1967

Lorenz, K., *King Solomon's Ring*, Reprint Society, 1953

McCroskey, Larson and Knapp, *Introduction to Interpersonal Behaviour*, Hall, Englewood Cliffs, 1971

MacHovec, F.J., *Body Talk*, Press, New York, 1975

Here's the letter I sent them:

```
Prentice Hall Inc.
U.S. Highway
9 Englewood Cliffs
NEW OORK
U.S.A.


Dear Sir

Enclosed is a copy of the book "Body Language ... How To
Read Others Thoughts By Their Gestures" published by
Allan Pease in Sydney Australia.  This book was
released on 15th December 1981 in this country and
has become an overnight success and is cureently
in it's fourth printing.  The fourth printing takes
the total numbers of books in this country to 27,000
which in relation to population is exceptional.

Mr Pease is a very personable Management Consultant
from North Sydney who has the unique ability to present
this subject in a rather remarkable way.  He has appeared
on every National network in this country in addition
to appearing in practically every newspaper and magazine.
(see news articles enclosed)

He plans to come to the United States this year to
promote the book and is interested in seeking a
publisher with the view to publishing the book
there.  Could you please contact us at your earliest
convenience if you are interested in considering
publishing this book in America.


Regards
```

I kept most of the replies I received, some of which are here :

Here are some responses from the 23 publishers that replied to me:

'This book doesn't suit our list/agenda.'
'It's entertaining but we don't see it working in the USA.'
'We've seen books like this and don't see anything unique about it.'
'Thank you, but no thanks.'
'Good luck elsewhere.'

The most memorable response was: 'Body Language *may apply to* Australians but it doesn't really apply to the British.'

Fifteen publishers sent me their printed reply card, 'Don't call us – we'll call you', and the rest didn't respond at all. I was disappointed and disheartened but was determined to follow through, despite what anyone said, thought or did. I decided to catch a plane to New York and personally knock on the doors of these publishers and convince them to buy Body Language. After three days of calling and door-knocking, I was getting nowhere fast. Most publishers wouldn't see me, and the few who did showed little interest. I'd hit a brick wall – 13 said 'Go away', 6 agreed to see me but only 3 editors actually turned up. On my 29th call, a small publisher who felt sorry for me told me to get a literary agent. He said that in the USA you need an agent and gave me a list of five names. At a base level, I felt comforted that I was playing the numbers game – I just prayed it would produce a result quicker.

Two agents said 'No', two didn't front for the appointment and the last – an agent called Aaron Priest – liked me and the tenacity I showed for my book. He said he'd see what he could do. After his seventh attempt to find a publisher who would agree to a deal, he secured a contract for US$10,000 with Bantam Books, one of the world's biggest publishers!

Giving up on your goal because you had a setback is like slashing your other three tyres because you had a flat.

Body Language went on to sell over 7 million copies, was translated into 51 languages, became the subject of 9 BBC Science programmes and a 9-part TV series on UK Channel 4 (hosted by Barb and me). It was the subject of television specials for National Geographic Channel and Discovery Channel and was (and still is) set as a course in universities, colleges and sales and management courses everywhere. I secured my own top-rating TV series on Body Language, *which I personally wrote and hosted. Eventually, Barb and I were invited to the Kremlin to address the top 300 politicians of the new Russia. By the age of 33, I had appeared on TV in 35 countries with* Body Language, *I had toured the UK, Europe and 26 states of the USA. Twenty years later, I had received a truckload of awards and accolades and Honorary Professor status at three international universities. The point here is that if I had quit after the first or fifth or fifteenth knockback – which is what most people do – * Body Language, *and all that followed, would never have happened. Statistically speaking, I knew it would succeed; it was just a matter of when. Do not give up early on your ideas.*

'Many of life's failures are people who did not realise how close they were to success when they gave up.'
Thomas Edison

Does luck play a part?

You may think that this was all a series of random chances that lead to a number-one bestseller, but it wasn't. I had decided that I would self-publish *Body Language* despite what anyone else said, thought or did, and my RAS set the Law of Attraction in motion. If this particular set of circumstances had not happened, another set of circumstances would have occurred. Either way, it would have been successful because I started by deciding **what** I would do, not **how** I'd do it. I developed a written plan with a deadline and took the first step. Importantly, if I'd listened to those who said it was a bad move, or those who said I knew nothing about writing or publishing, or that the book market was tough, or that I should spend the $7,000 on a great holiday, my children's education or a new car, or that I should stick to what I knew, then *Body Language* would never have happened. Instead, my RAS located people who were successful writers and publishers and I asked them what I should do and how they did it themselves. I thanked my naysayer friends and relatives for their concerns and interest and proceeded with my plans.

**'Those who say it cannot be done
should not interrupt the one who is doing it.'
Chinese proverb**

Twenty-five years later, and after another eight number-one bestsellers, Barbara and I co-wrote *The Definitive Book of Body Language*, and despite 'experts' saying it was 'old hat' and 'out of vogue' it went on to hit the bestseller lists again everywhere. It continues to sell and sell and sell today.

Summary

Most people who struggle with success in life either won't ask for what they want or give up early.

When you believe you have an idea that's a winner, stick with it until you have exhausted every possible option before considering what to do next. Tell everyone about your ideas and plans and ask them to help you.

Don't give up. The beginning is always the hardest part. If you feel like quitting, reread your goal list and think only about what you want as your outcome.

Never let the odds keep you from doing what you know in your heart you were meant to do.

Go as far as you can see and when you get there you'll be able to see further than you could at the start. Go the extra mile – it's never crowded.

Some succeed because they are destined to, but most succeed because they are determined to.

Whatever venture or course you decide to take in life, only ask for opinions from those who have experienced your situation, who are where you want to be, or who have expertise in what you want. When it comes to your goals, take advice only from people who have done or are doing what you intend to do. Other people's opinions are just opinions and can often be destructive and unhelpful.

- Go after what you want or you'll never have it.
- Ask, ask, ask – or the answer will always be 'No'.
- Step forward or you will always be in the same place.
- Failure doesn't come from falling down. Failure comes from not getting up.

Never give in – never, never, never, never, in nothing great or small, large or petty. Never give in except to convictions of honour and good sense. Never yield to force; never yield to the apparently overwhelming might of the enemy.'
Winston Churchill

Chapter 14

From the Outhouse to the Penthouse

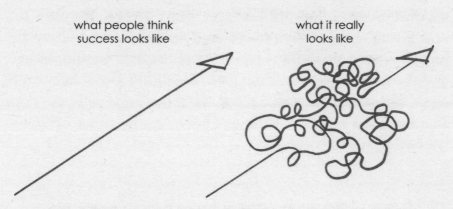

what people think
success looks like

what it really
looks like

Barbara and I debated whether or not to include these next two chapters in this book. They are autobiographical and personal to us both, but we decided to do so because they demonstrate how we have applied the principles in *The Answer* to our own lives.

After 15 years of global success with the *Body Language* series of books, the subsequent TV series and documentaries, life was good. We owned prestige cars, a large ocean cruiser, a beautiful home on the water, and a country retreat; we travelled to exotic destinations; and we had buckets of fame and glory.

In 1994, Barbara and I became the victims of bad judgement – our own bad judgement. We lost everything – our home, investments, cash and self-esteem. After years of huge success, everything disappeared almost overnight and we were left with debts in the millions. Following another two years of lawyers and accountants, misery, depression, paying back the debts and my getting cancer as a result of the stress, we decided to start again. It was a daunting time because we had exhausted the market for *Body Language* books and products, I was 45 and Barb was 34 – and we were broke. This was when we made the irreversible decision to become more successful than we had ever been before. We then sat at a plastic card table a friend had loaned us and wrote by hand our new goals. We detailed the lifestyle we would live and the success we would achieve. We didn't know *how* we'd do it, but we had decided *what* we'd do, and we knew that was the most important thing. There was no other option – we had to move forward.

**Good judgement comes from bad experience.
And most of that comes from bad judgement.**

After more months of soul-searching, we decided that our plan would be to write new books that would sell in the millions instead of the tens or hundreds of thousands as they had previously done. This clearly defined goal meant we now had to think in other ways about how to write books if we were to make this leap up. We decided to only write books that people would want to buy without having to be convinced – books they'd want even if they didn't know who we were.

Following the international success of *Body Language* in the 1970s and 1980s, we wrote books that people really needed such as my *How to Write Letters and Emails that Get Results* and Barbara's *How to Remember Names and Faces*. These books were Top Ten bestsellers and sold hundreds of thousands of copies, but in order for us to make a financial comeback, this approach was too limiting. While everyone will agree that improving your ability to remember people's names is important, they never consider buying a book about it. Everyone agrees that the ability to communicate in writing is essential – but they don't search out a book on how to do it. You have to sell them the idea of buying it. But people will buy a book about how to get more money, love, power and sex. And so this would be the answer for us.

We had written books about the things people really needed, not what they really wanted.

We would now only write books about these things – the topics readers would pay us money to read about. We'd use *their* preferences, not *ours*. By clearly stating our new goals in writing, the RAS went into search mode. We immediately started to see new titles to write about and ways of writing we'd never considered.

Programming the RAS to a high level the way we did was dramatic because it's presumptuous to decide to write only Top Ten bestsellers. We had to do it this way, though, because I was 45 and didn't want to reach the age of 70 and still be paying off a home. If we hadn't been in such dismal circumstances we may never have set our goals so high, but we didn't have any choice. What happened as a result shows how powerful the RAS is when you use it correctly.

Authors are rarely good at making business decisions, so we decided to make all future decisions from a business standpoint first. This way our decisions would be financially sensible. While most authors write about their personal expertise or passions, we decided we would be business people first – everything else would be secondary.

The formation of our next big book

When you are broke and have nothing left you are forced to examine what you really want from life. After nearly three years of trying to climb out of our financial hole, Barb's and my relationship was under serious pressure. If you've been in a long-term relationship with someone you'll identify with where we were. '*You can't live with them, but you can't live without them.*'

Our main issues were the usual ones most couples experience – the differences between how men and women perceive life. To try to resolve these issues and to avoid separation or divorce, we decided to write a list of the things about each other that we found hard to live with. We figured that if we could resolve, compromise or negotiate these things, we could live a happy life together. Most men can make a list of six to eight things that bother them about their partners – I had six on my list. But I had to stop Barbara writing her list when she reached page four! My complaint list included Barb's inability to read road maps, not getting to the point, talking when I needed silence, waffling, not having sex with me as often as I wanted – all typical male complaints. Her list included my not asking for directions, solving her 'problems' when she just wanted me to listen, telling her how to think, wanting too much sex, and leaving the toilet seat up. While we didn't realise it at the time, these lists would form the basis of one of our next bestsellers, which we tentatively called 'Relationship Rescue'.

**Friendships between women:
A woman doesn't come home one night. The next day she tells her husband that she slept over at a girlfriend's house. He calls his wife's ten best friends. None of them knows anything about it.**

**Friendships between men:
A man doesn't come home one night.
The next day he tells his wife that he slept over at a friend's house. She calls her husband's ten best friends. Eight of them confirm he slept over, two claim he's still there.**

With our new goals and plans crystallised in writing, we decided that Australia wasn't large enough for us to reach these goals. We'd need to find larger markets to crack the big time. We needed to go to countries with sizeable populations to sell large numbers of books and to speak at huge conferences. We then tackled the scary part of our ambitious plan – we set a deadline. We decided that within 12 months we would be established and operating in Europe.

Standing on top of the world

We bought a large map of the world for $15, laid it out on our living-room floor and stood over it. We decided that there were only two big world markets for us – the USA or Europe. Europe seemed like a better option because it had a bigger population. Including Russia and the other Eastern European countries, Europe had around 1 billion people compared to 300 million in the USA. Europe was easier to get around than the USA and was a more mysterious and exciting place for us. The Berlin Wall was being pulled down and Communism in Eastern Europe was coming to an end. We decided to tackle the unknown in these new markets and to become well-known identities.

We determined that England was the logical country to be based in because we spoke the language. We would live somewhere in the centre, close to the motorways and near an international airport so we could travel easily. We took a pin and put it in the middle of the map of England. It landed on a tiny town called Henley-in-Arden, in Warwickshire.

**The darkest room often holds
the greatest treasure.**

We had never heard of Henley-in-Arden, we knew nothing about it and knew no-one who lived there. We had absolutely no idea how things would unfold, we just knew what we wanted to do and Henley-in-Arden was in the approximate centre of England. We had decided the **what** and fed it to the RAS – we trusted that the **how** would soon show itself.

Entering the unknown

Going to the UK with only a goal and our faith in the universe was both scary and exciting. We agreed that Barb would be the driving force behind generating income – she would call big companies and sell me in as a speaker at their conferences. On reflection, it seems almost impossible that we could have done what we did, but we had no other choice. When your back is up against a wall, there is a sword in your hand and you have no other options, you can only move forward. We refused to even contemplate anything other than success. We were going to make it back bigger than ever. End of story. And we would follow through with our plan despite what anyone said, thought or did.

The road ahead materialises

At a conference in Hong Kong two years earlier, we had met a speaker named John Fenton. He lived in Warwickshire and had said, 'If you are ever in Warwickshire, come and stay at my place.' It was the kind of invitation you might make to people you meet and get on well with, but you never really expect them to turn up. However, he lived near Henley-in-Arden so we decided to accept his offer. It would be polite to phone him first and tell him in advance we were coming, so I called him. 'Hi John, remember us? We accept your invitation. Put the kettle on – we're coming over next week!'

The phone went silent. Then he said, 'Okay…come on over!' When you have clearly defined goals and ask others for help, many people want to assist you. We asked clearly for what we wanted and got a 'Yes'. We felt the direct approach was better as it didn't give John the chance to refuse – and we needed somewhere to stay. If John had said 'No' we would have gone to plan B, whatever that was!

When you set clearly defined goals you begin to act and talk positively and directly about what you want and what you will do.

Arriving in Henley-in-Arden

One week later, on 10 May 1997, we boarded a plane in Sydney, having bought two super-cheap tickets to the UK with our last $2,000, and landed at Heathrow airport at 5 a.m. We rented a small car, and drove two hours to what would soon become our home, the tiny Shakespearian village of Henley-in-Arden, Warwickshire.

John Fenton is retired now and has been able to slow down, but when we met him he was a gregarious, dynamic man. He had written several sales books, ran his own motivational seminars and was a successful property developer. He was the type of guy who was so full of energy that, after you'd spent an hour with him, you needed to take a week off to get over it. He is also a caring and generous person. We arrived at John's home in Warwickshire and, over dinner, explained to him what had happened to us and why we were there. He was both amazed and impressed.

'So you just decided to turn up on the other side of the world where no-one knows you, you don't know anyone, you're broke, you'll write only bestsellers and make it big? Is that what you're telling me?' he asked.

'That's a perfect summary, John!' I said.

He looked down, put his hands over his face, shook his head and, laughing, said, 'Then we'd better have a drink to celebrate!'

He opened a bottle of champagne and before long we were all falling about, laughing at the absurdity of it all.

As Barb and I watched the sun rise over Henley-in-Arden the next morning, we were struck by the reality and enormity of what we were about to do.

'So...what books are you going to write and how will you sell them?' John asked over breakfast.

'That's a technical detail, John,' I said. 'But we'll work out what to do and we'll do it better than anyone has ever done it! We've decided what we'll do and that's the biggest decision.'

'Where will you live?' John continued.

'That's a technical detail too, John,' I laughed. 'Do you have any suggestions?'

One of the exciting things about setting big goals and telling others about them is that many people want to try to help you achieve them. John Fenton was excited about the idea of being part of what some people saw as an impossible dream.

First we needed somewhere to live, so John introduced us to Tony Earl, a conservative, 60-year-old man in a tweed jacket. Tony ran the real estate agency that his father had started in Henley-in-Arden in 1920. We shared our experiences with Tony and his staff and explained how we had ended up in his office. He sat there and stared at us curiously, as someone might study chimpanzees in a zoo.

'So you put a pin in a map...it landed on my office... and now you're here to do business and to live?' he asked.

'But you have no money, nowhere to stay and no work…?'

'Exactly!' I said. 'But we will have these things soon, Tony, that's why we've come to see you. How can you help us?'

Tony laughed. In fact, everyone at that meeting laughed. He then treated us to lunch and joked that this could be our 'last supper'.

Despite all the laughter, everyone was impressed that we had the determination to do this after what we'd been through and that we had such ambitious, almost outrageous plans. Over the next two days we developed a good relationship with Tony and he showed us properties that were available for sale and rental to give us a feel for Henley-in-Arden. The best we could find in rental accommodation cost £800 a month (A$2,000). On top of that we'd have to buy furniture, office equipment, telephones and, somehow, a car before we could get started. It seemed almost impossible because we had no money. But when you are driven toward your goals and use your RAS, answers appear. By the third day of going nowhere, Tony put his hands on our shoulders and in a concerned, fatherly way, asked, 'Are you sure this is really what you want to do with your lives?'

'Absolutely, Tony! We've decided what we want…we're just not sure how we'll do it yet.'

Even though I was upbeat about it all, Barbara and I went back to John's place despondent because we still had nowhere to live. 'Something will turn up, honey,' I reassured her. 'It always does.'

Stars can't shine without darkness.

While Barb had undying faith in my determination to work out what to do, she must have also thought I was a bit nutty.

Not only had she also lost everything financially since we met, she now had the job of running a new business on the other side of the world with nowhere to live and a man who had no money, only dreams. But I figured that with the kind of support I had from her and the love we had for each other, success for us was inevitable, one way or the other. What was the worst that could happen? I knew that even if we had to sleep in a barn with animals, Barb would be prepared to do it. And if, in the end, we only had each other, life would still be worth it. Besides, I had successfully used goal-setting all my life and regularly headed into the unknown. This was really the same – just a lot bigger. Some people called this the Law of Attraction, the universe or God – we knew it to be the RAS.

Early one morning, Tony rang and asked us to see him. Like John, he'd become wrapped up in the Pease Crazy Adventure Tour and was enjoying being part of it.

He explained that he owned a 17th-century watermill just outside Henley-in-Arden and that it was currently vacant. He said the watermill was fully equipped for living and had a basement that – with a bit of tidying up – could be used as an office. He said he'd charge us a nominal rent of £500 a month and we could pay him later when we got on our feet and had the money. We were over the moon! We had our start!

Ask, ask, ask!

**When you are clear about what you want
and ask for help, you'll get it, even from
people you haven't met yet.**

Tony and John told everyone in the village the story of the two crazy Australians who went broke, put a pin in a map, turned up in Henley-in-Arden with nothing and were now living in Tony's watermill. John said that he had a conference coming up with over 2,000 attendees, and he would put me on the speaking program. Also, he'd lend us a car. When we'd boarded that plane in Sydney seven days earlier, we knew no one in the UK other than John. We had only our goals, a deadline, determination, each other, and a small rental car. Now we were living in a fully equipped home, had a potential office, two new best friends, a car and a job! The RAS always works...

You may be thinking we were simply lucky to find John and Tony, but that's not true. We had a clearly defined goal and would only consider success. If we had not met John and Tony, we would have met two other people in another town and some other 'lucky' events would have happened. Luck is what happens when you don't have a clear goal and are not expecting anything. For us, luck was never part of our plan.

**'Be careful what you wish for as it will
eventually come to pass.'
Julius Caesar**

The birth of our European business

Tony's watermill was located next to a cemetery in the tiny village of Wootton Wawen, population 186, just outside Henley-in-Arden. There was a water race at the back that was originally used to turn a waterwheel for grinding grain.

Tony gave us a bedroom on the third floor and we set up our office in the basement, which was a 5-by-5-metre cold, mouldy room that hadn't been used since the 19th century, but to us it was beautiful. The damp, cold and mould were irrelevant. We were excited that we had a place to call home and a base to operate from, however bad it smelled.

With our last $800, we visited an office liquidation store in a country barn and did a deal to buy two desks, three chairs and a filing cabinet. We told the store owner our story and asked what he could do to help us. He said that he and his wife had also recovered from a financial disaster and he was so impressed with our venture that he threw in desk calendars, floor mats, office accessories and free delivery to help us get started. As we've said continually, when you set clearly defined goals and ask others to help you, people will

The Old Watermill in Wootton Wawen near Stratford-on-Avon.

respond, even those you haven't met yet.

We had brought our laptops with us from Australia and John lent us a car, two telephones and a *Yellow Pages* phone book. We were ready for action! And to think that, ten days earlier, we had not even heard of Wootton Wawen. Our clearly defined goals were handwritten on a list in Barbara's handbag and we had the determination to follow through, despite what anyone might say, think or do. That night, in our mouldy cellar, we opened a bottle of supermarket wine and toasted the opening of Pease International UK. It felt surreal. None of our friends or family had any idea where we were, what we were doing or that we were on the other side of the world. It felt like we were on another planet. At nine o'clock the next morning, Barb sat at her second-hand desk, opened the *Yellow Pages* at A – assurance companies – picked up the phone and started dialling.

Sticking with it

The first two months saw Barb relentlessly calling the training directors of big assurance companies, trying to sell me into their next conference as a keynote speaker, while I ploughed away at constructing our next book.

Establishing ourselves in another country proved to be much harder than we had ever imagined. Even though many Australians share British heritage, the Brits think differently from Australians and business is conducted in different ways from what Barb and I knew. It's not what you know as much as who you know – and we only knew John, Tony and the guy at the furniture store. It was a dead-cold start for us.

Along with the UK, Europe would be our biggest market and that meant we would either have to learn new languages or hire multilingual staff. We signed up for German-language tuition and I set a goal to be competent enough deliver a speech in French to a French audience.

After three months, Barb had secured two conference spots for me in the UK. After that we returned to Australia to fulfil commitments and tidy up loose ends. We then waited in Australia for one of the clients to pay their deposit so we had enough money to buy plane tickets back to Wootton Wawen.

An arrow can only be shot by pulling it backward. So when life seems to be dragging you back with difficulties, it's really about to launch you into something great.

In that first year we travelled back and forth from Australia to the UK four times and slowly, bit by bit, we built a list of British fans and clients, while our European business also started to take shape. The first conferences I spoke at were with assurance companies, banks and computer firms because A, B and C are at the start of the *Yellow Pages*. We told everyone about our plans and asked them to help us, and, like a raging bushfire, word of us began to spread. People began appearing from everywhere and they either wanted to ride on our roller coaster or watch it crash and burn.

In the late 1980s, I had appeared on several British TV shows with scientists who were demonstrating the differences between men's and women's brains using the new MRI technology. At that time, my conference presentations were on the topic of how to present ideas differently to men and women. While it was well received at seminars, this idea was also controversial because it was seen as politically incorrect to say that men and women were not equally capable of doing certain things. Barb thought this topic was perfect for our next book because of the controversy about the subject material. Also, it was clearly something everyone needed to understand. After much debate and discussion between us, we decided to develop our next book on the science of men, women and relationships. We had our personal lists that we had written about each other; they would form the basis of this new manuscript.

> **'We are all faced with a series of great opportunities brilliantly disguised as impossible situations.'**
> **Charles Swindoll, author of *Insight for Living***

The title for our new book came to us in Italy when we were running late to catch a plane at Milan airport. I was driving the rental car and Barb was reading the map. Well, reading the map is an exaggeration. She was rotating it from left to right and upside down, trying to get it to match the surrounding Italian landscape while, at the same time, urging me to stop and ask for directions. The result was an argument that all couples know. I complained that if she would learn to read maps properly, we wouldn't keep getting lost. She countered that if I'd learn to listen rather than criticise – and to stop to ask for directions – we wouldn't be lost in the first place! The argument became so heated that she told me to stop on the motorway and she hailed a cab to the airport. As I followed the cab in the little Fiat rental car, I watched her waving to me through the back window of the cab, but she wasn't using all five fingers. After this Italian experience we arrived at the title for our book, *Why Men Don't Listen and Women Can't Read Maps*. We would write about the differences between men and women, back it all up with scientific evidence and real stories, and it would be as funny as hell! We believed that no-one had ever written anything like this.

While Barb continued to canvass the As, Bs and Cs of the *Yellow Pages*, I would speak at seminars and at night we would read and reread the evolving manuscript. Two years later, in 1998, it was ready. We cracked open another bottle of champagne in our watermill and toasted the future.

We were driving down the M40 motorway in England with the manuscript, and I said calmly to Barb, 'This is it, babe! This is our comeback! We are going to the top!' We knew we had a hit!

In Portofino, Italy, when we came up with the title *Why Men Don't Listen and Women Can't Read Maps*.

Our plan of action

We decided to self-publish *Why Men Don't Listen and Women Can't Read Maps* to maximise our profits. We released it in Australia first because, although Australia is not a big market, we could push it into the bestseller lists quickly and use that credibility to sell it into the bigger international book markets. We were going to need lots of media exposure, and our formula to achieve it was to do the journalists' work for them. If you are an author you should never wait to be discovered – write the articles and give them to the media. We created our own headlines, stories and themes then gave them to the appropriate journalists. Our stories were always controversial, provocative – or both – and would usually go against the current politically correct thinking. This was at the time of the height of political correctness, when it was fashionable for people to pretend that men and women thought the same way. We returned to Australia, wrote our press releases and launched *Why Men Don't Listen and Women Can't Read Maps*. We sent press releases with headlines like:

Why women can't find their way out of a paper bag
Why Australian men are clueless lovers
Why women can't reverse-park
Why men can only do one thing at a time
Why women never stop talking
Why men don't marry feminists.

We knew that being politically incorrect would stir up media attention. And being controversial is an important way to become well known. Most authors, musicians, artists and actors sit around waiting for the big-break phone call, which rarely comes. We wanted to be at the helm of our own ship and to sail it where we wanted it to go, regardless of which way the wind was blowing.

Take charge. Don't wait to be discovered.

We quickly found that the Australian feminists would come after me with a baseball bat and that whatever I said, they'd want to shoot it down. But we also discovered that if Barbara said the same things – *exactly* the same things – the feminists were generally okay with it or even impressed by it. So we developed a good guy/bad guy routine, with me as the provoker and Barb as the pacifier. This worked well for us because instead of taking the attacks from the feminists personally, we used them to push *Why Men Don't Listen and Women Can't Read Maps* into everyone's face, and the public loved it. Within a month, *Why Men Don't Listen and Women Can't Read Maps* hit number one in the Australian bestseller list. It held the number-one position for three months and sold over 50,000 copies. We were back in business!

The Hit List TOP 10 BOOKS

PREVIOUS WEEK'S POSITION AFTER TITLE		WEEKS IN RELEASE*
1 **Why Men Don't Listen ...** (1)	Allan & Barbara Pease	3
2 **The Sound of One Hand ...** (3)	Richard Flannagan	3
3 **The Color of Water** (7)	James McBride	57
4 **Angela's Ashes** (6)	Frank McCourt	102
5 **Rainbow Six** (2)	Tom Clancy	6
6 **Memoirs of a Geisha** (10)	Arthur Golden	7
7 **Believe and Achieve** (4)	Paul Hanna	4
8 **A Monk Swimming** (5)	Malachy McCourt	12
9 **Point of Origin** (–)	Patricia Cornwell	12
10 **Deja Dead** (–)	Kathy Reichs	3

WEEK ENDING SEPT. 20. *IN CURRENT FORMAT.
SOURCE: DYMOCKS BOOKSELLERS

Handling obstacles and roadblocks

After our Australian success, we shopped our manuscript to many UK publishers but they showed no interest. It was a familiar story – they didn't know us, didn't know the subject area and it was all too hard for them. They said our ideas might work in Australia but the British wouldn't go for it. So we set a goal to create our own book distribution business in Britain and to take control of our market. We were determined to follow through with our plans despite what others might say, think or do. We soon discovered that book distribution in the UK is like the publishing business – a closed shop, filled with people who all knew each other. Once again, the problem was that no-one knew us and self-published authors were not seen as cool.

Barb set a goal to become the best friend of the three biggest book distributors in the UK. She called them weekly, sent them notes, offered ideas, and 'camped out' with them for so long that they became used to having her around. She also called every high-profile journalist in the UK and befriended a journalist with the *Daily Mail* who loved our book and agreed to run a three-day serial in that influential newspaper. It's important to understand that when the *Daily Mail* agreed to run our series, Barb had received 18 knockbacks from other major newspapers and magazines. She was playing the Numbers Game.

As part of our plan, Barb and I phoned the major UK bookstores every day asking if they had the new Pease book on their shelves. Obviously they didn't – they'd never heard of it. But we created a demand by getting the bookstores to ask the distributors if they had our books. Gradually, the bookstores began to order – 10 copies here, 20 there, and the occasional

50 copies. Barb would package these books and walk them to the post office every day. Eventually, she convinced a book distributor, Jim, to give us the break we needed. He had heard about our story from several bookstores and had read the *Daily Mail* serial, and he wanted to give us a leg-up. Barb had been ringing him regularly for six months and he was also becoming inundated with calls from bookstores that wanted to find this new book with its contemptible title. Jim agreed to take 500 books on consignment as a test run. But if it didn't sell, he warned, we'd all look bad and the stores would send the books back. Barb was devastated. She was already personally selling more than this amount directly to the bookstores!

Jim's first 500 copies sold out on the first day. So he took another 2,000 copies. They sold out in under a week. Within three months, we were bestselling authors in Britain.

Barb with her parents at our new British home, Umberslade Hall.

Our new home

We found a beautiful apartment on the top floor of a converted 17th-century stately home that was on the market for A$400,000. It was owned by an elderly couple, Maisey and Eric. We offered them a 5 per cent deposit (that's all we had so far) and said we'd pay the balance in 12 months when the money came in from our book sales. They had heard about our story from Tony, the real estate agent, and they'd read about us in the newspapers. We asked for their help to finance us for a year, and they said 'Yes'. They were also excited by our plans, and 12 months later we owned our first British home! We lived here for the next five years and eventually became the biggest shareholders in this magnificent historic building. Called Umberslade Hall, it is just outside Henley-in-Arden, exactly where our pin had landed on the map three years earlier.

Never giving up

There were many days when things looked bleak or didn't go our way. But when you have clearly defined goals, you are motivated by looking toward the final outcome, not the obstacle in front of you. Without goals, people are motivated by the roadblocks that appear in front of them or what happens to them next. Statistically, most 'next' things that happen don't produce results. When you start on a new goal, the 80/20 rule means that 80 per cent of what you initially do won't produce results.

We constantly called the big TV and radio shows and gave them ideas about stimulating and entertaining segments, and we soon became regulars on British television. This success led to us being involved in nine major TV documentaries and our own ten-part series based on our books. We were now hot property! Barb convinced a large UK publisher to be our distribution arm, and after six months of success they offered us A$1,000,000 to publish *Why Men Don't Listen and Women Can't Read Maps*.

We were both amazed and delighted with this offer, but we thought that if it was worth a million to them, we could do it ourselves and make ten times that. Remember, our major goal was to become financially independent again. If that had not been our goal, we might have taken the money. We were now British publishers.

Instead of thinking outside the box, get rid of the box.

The *Daily Mail* journalist was thrilled to be part of our roller-coaster ride and was keen to help us even more. Six months later, she introduced us to British-American literary agent Dorie Simmonds, who she said could sell us and our books to foreign publishers. The Pease–Simmonds partnership went on to sell more than 20 million books over the next ten years, with translations into 54 languages, and we produced another seven bestsellers. We toured the world like rock stars for the next decade – visiting 20 to 30 countries every year – and we attracted tens of millions of fans. We were now living the life we had visualised the day we stood on the map of the world in our little Sydney house and set our new goals.

During this wild time we also had a number-one box-office movie in Europe, titled *Warum Männer Nicht Zuhären und*

Frauen Schlecht Einparken (*Why Men Don't Listen and Women Can't Park Cars*). It was also shown on television across Europe and became a stage show, playing in Paris, Lyon, Rome, Prague and Amsterdam.

Woche Rang Titel		Verl.	29.11-05.12 Woche
1	WARUM MÄNNER NICHT ZUHÄREN...	CON	1,542,227
2	AMERICAN GANGSTER	UPI	1,011,695
3	SCHWERTER D. KÄNIGS-DUNGEON S.	FOX	878,900
4	NACH 7 TAGEN - AUSGEFLITTERT	UPI	497,312

We developed a global monthly advice column that, at its peak, had over 20 million readers. In 2005, we had five titles in the European bestseller lists and were the world's biggest-selling non-fiction authors and second overall globally to J. K. Rowling's *Harry Potter*. We had come a long way from

Some of our books had difficulty reaching the number-one position because our other books already held that spot. Barb was invited to the German Book Fair in Leipzig and received an award for our first 1,000,000 books sold in the German language.

our cockroach-ridden little house in Sydney and being faced with bankruptcy.

Why Men Don't Listen and Women Can't Read Maps went on to sell over 12 million copies. The sequel, *Why Men Don't Have a Clue and Women Need More Shoes*, sold over three million copies. *The Definitive Book of Body Language* sold over two million and *Questions are the Answers* sold two million. Including the pirated, published editions of our books in Russian, Chinese, Indian, Indonesian and other languages, there are now an estimated 60 million Pease books in circulation.

It's important to understand that we have written here about the enormous success we achieved globally. But for every successful forward step, we often got knocked three steps back. The results we have described here account for about 20 per cent of our initial efforts – the other 80 per cent of what we attempted got zero results. We played the numbers game, had handwritten, clearly defined goals and deadlines. We constantly visualised the outcomes we wanted and used affirmations daily. Doing this, asking people for help, and making the decision to follow through despite what others say, think or do – gets results.

Entering Russia

In 1990, we wrote down a goal to crack the world's greatest untapped yet huge potential market – Russia. We planned we would go to Russia, associate with high-level people and become public identities. At first, we put it on our C list without a deadline because you couldn't get a visa to go there. When we set this goal in 1990, the USSR was Communist and was behind the Iron Curtain. It was close to impossible to travel there, let alone publish a book or speak at a conference. To us, though, it was exciting because no Western speakers or authors had done it. Also, Russia carried with it images of spies, espionage and the KGB – all the James Bond stuff – so we added it to our C list.

When we mentioned this goal to others, many people gave us reasons why it was unrealistic and would be a waste of energy even trying to go there. They mentioned the Cold War, the Iron Curtain, how Westerners mysteriously disappeared there, the Mafia, the KGB, we'd probably be robbed, murdered and have our kidneys stolen. We would thank them for their input, acknowledge the truth or their right to have an opinion, and then let the RAS continue to search for answers.

From the moment the Russian goal was written, we began to see information about Russia everywhere – on TV, in the newspapers and magazines – and we began to hear Russian accents around us. If we hadn't programmed this goal into the RAS, we would never have seen or heard anything Russian. When President Gorbachev dissolved the USSR on 25 December 2001, our C goal suddenly loomed as a reality. We moved it to the B list and set a deadline to be established in Russia within two years.

A ship in port is safe, but that's not what ships are built for.

In January 1992 we were at a Chamber of Commerce function in Sydney when Barbara heard a Russian accent somewhere behind us. There were about 200 people at that function, but because the Russian goal was written on our list, her ears detected this accent. Otherwise she never would have heard it above all the noise. That's how the RAS works. We introduced ourselves to Alexandri, a Russian man who was in Australia to look for ideas to take to the new Russia. Barb and I enthusiastically sold him the idea of publishing *Body Language* in Russia and taking us there for a seminar and media tour. It was an easy sale for us to make because we had been mentally rehearsing this moment for over two years.

After two weeks of discussions and negotiations, we reached an agreement. We would teach Alexandri how to publish a book and how to run a public event with a PR campaign. In return, he would find sponsors to fund the project and we would split the profits. Alexandri's plan was to start our 'road show' with a PR campaign in Moscow and our first seminar in St Petersburg and then travel by train to Gorky, back to Moscow, and beyond. We were warned by others that we might never be paid a rouble of any profits, but we really wanted to do it – so we proceeded! Russian currency could not be exchanged or transferred at that time, so Alexandri agreed to pay our share of the profits with vodka and black caviar. We'd ship this produce in trucks to the UK and sell it there to recover our share.

Having fun with the KGB

The KGB had been disbanded by the time we first flew into Moscow from Australia and former KGB agents were readily available for hire as security guards for US$10 a day. We hired three. Their job was to protect us and to negotiate with the local Mafia in each city for our safety and security. We had up to eleven people in our entourage – bodyguards, TV crew, PR agent, Barb, Alexandri, myself and Barb's father, Bill, who would be our 'gofer'. The Russians all smoked, drank vodka and carried guns. I jokingly told Alexandri that Barbara and I were the only ones who didn't have guns. He was very embarrassed about it and said he'd get one for us in the next city! In Moscow, he sold us onto major Russian TV talk shows and other big media, and then we boarded the train to Leningrad, recently renamed St Petersburg.

Throughout March 1992 we toured Russia like celebrities, giving seminars to huge crowds and appearing on TV and in the media everywhere. The seminars were filmed and later produced as a TV series that was broadcast every Saturday for over a year, attracting a Russian-speaking audience of around 70 million. Our first Russian print run of *Body Language* was a million copies and it sold out in four weeks, so Alexandri immediately printed another million copies. We soon became the best-known authors in Russia.

'Take me to the Kremlin'

After the collapse of Communism, we studied the behaviour of Russian politicians who appeared on international television. The media interest in them was high due to the dramatic changes taking place in Russia, but because of the lack of any media training these politicians came across to the outside world as aggressive, clumsy and inept. Our plan was to convince them that it was essential to make good first impressions when they met other world leaders, and that they needed our help. We wanted the new President, Boris Yeltsin, to be our first Russian student but Alexandri said he was too unpredictable and unreliable. We would do better to run a media training conference for other, more co-operative, high-profile politicians. After a number of failed attempts to find a suitable politician to train, Alexandri said he had a friend who knew the new governor of St Petersburg, Anatoly Sobchak. Sobchak was the first democratically elected politician in Russia and was seen as progressive. Alexandri contacted him to float our idea and he loved it! If you can't get help from the first person, ask the next – and the next. Sobchak arranged for 300 new politicians to attend a conference we titled *How to be Credible in the World Media* to be held at the Kremlin. Only top politicians and dignitaries would attend, including Sobchak's new deputy, former KGB officer Vladimir Putin.

From another 'impossible' goal that was written on our

On the sleeper train to Gorky: Barb, her father Bill, our Russian agents, lots of vodka, guns, and minus 10 degrees Celsius outside.

Alexandri, Barb, Bill and our Russian entourage. Can you pick which four of these people are carrying a gun?

C list two years earlier, we had become TV celebrities in the new Russia, travelling with our own KGB agents and Vladimir Putin was waiting for us in the Kremlin. This was *better* than a James Bond movie!

We arrived at the Kremlin and went to a magnificent gold Stalinist theatre where the seminar would be held. When Vladimir Putin walked in he was not the overwhelming figure we had expected to see. He was a lean, solemn-looking man, but his presence commanded attention from everyone in the room. Putin had been a senior mover in the KGB and had a reputation for being someone who did what was necessary to get the job done. His new role as deputy mayor was his opening to enter politics and move to higher levels.

Our conference that day was an outstanding success and the Russians learned how to come across positively in front of the TV cameras and to gain acceptance from the rest of the world.

We didn't realise it at the time, but we were fortunate to be witnessing an historical turning point for Russia, its politicians and its people. Today we spend around three months a year in Russia and it is our biggest conference market.

Summary

The RAS is such a powerful tool that it can take you anywhere you want to go. It's your personal GPS. All you need to do is first decide what goals you'd like to achieve and write them down. List them from **A** to **C**, and create deadlines for the A-list items. When the hows begin to appear around you, develop them into a plan. Then move forward despite what others may think, say or do. Learn the new habits you'll need to make your journey easier, develop positive affirmations, and use visualisation. And whatever happens along the way, see the humorous side of things. That's what Barb and I have always done because we know it works. And it will work for you as soon as you decide to use it.

A
_____
_____
_____
_____
_____
_____
_____

B
_____
_____
_____
_____
_____
_____
_____
_____

C
_____
_____
_____
_____
_____
_____
_____

Chapter 15

Tell Your Body
What to Do

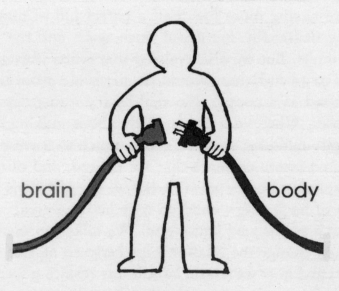

brain   body

The brain's ability to instruct the body to achieve remarkable outcomes is well researched and documented. The story you are about to read shows the power of the RAS and highlights the lessons in this book. These events happened to Barbara and me personally, and they produced an outcome unlike anything we have ever experienced.

Two years after my diagnosis and treatment for prostate cancer, and in the face of almost impossible odds, Barb and I decided to have more children. Family members were stunned by this decision and some were at a loss to comprehend why we'd choose this goal in view of our circumstances and ages. I was 52 and had no viable sperm because of radiation treatment I'd received for prostate cancer. Barb was 41, which is medically geriatric in terms of conception. We jointly had four kids from previous marriages – two girls and two boys. This was a momentous decision that we knew would dramatically alter the course of our lives. We had spent the past 15 years travelling the world, were bestselling authors in many countries and were having more fun than a barrel full of monkeys. We were financially successful once again and the future had no limits. But we also realised that when it eventually all came to an end, there would be no visible proof that we ever existed as a couple. No real legacy – just cars, cash and houses. When your life is solely about making money and empire-building, you don't have much to leave behind. We wanted future evidence that we existed, and our name on a hospital or library wasn't what we wanted. This is why the idea of having new children together had great appeal, so we set it as our next major goal. We talked through how this would change the relationships between all our family members and how we would handle any resulting scenarios. Some family members were dead against the idea and most of our friends were dumbfounded. But for us, this was **the answer** to many of our needs as a couple. We decided that we would put ourselves first above everyone and everything and take this path despite what anyone said, thought or did. The first obstacle, however, was that it would be near-impossible – statistically speaking – that it could happen. But we had decided **what** we wanted, knowing that the **how** would soon reveal itself.

Here's a note from a diary I had been keeping at the time:

2 December 2002, Spain

We've decided to have more kids – how's that for ambition? Me without a prostate, I've had radiation and a vasectomy and Barb over 40! Now this will be a real test of goal-setting! We're working out how to do it – we think we'll have two girls – the path is not clear yet. If necessary, we may even use a surrogate. Worst-case scenario, we'll adopt. This will be the beginning of our new life for the next 40 years. We don't know how we'll do it yet, we just know we'll do it somehow and that's what counts most.

Round I

On our list we wrote our clearly defined goal, in handwriting – *To have two new healthy children.* We searched the Internet, looking at everything about conception. We consulted fertility doctors, gynaecologists and urologists to establish how we were going to achieve this physically doubtful goal. It was disappointing to read the many stories about healthy, younger couples who had attempted to conceive and had failed. Next we consulted IVF experts, who were pessimistic and said our chances of success were extremely low. And if I couldn't produce any viable sperm, forget it. One urologist said, 'You're going to die of cancer anyway, Allan, so why do you want to have kids?' This comment added to the overall disrespect Barb and I had developed for the medical profession during my cancer treatment.

Some of our friends and relatives said we were being irresponsible even considering having children at our age, especially in view of my cancer record. Others pointed out that even if it could work, when our new children were 21, I would be 76 and Barb would be 65. So we sidelined all the doctors, relatives and others who seemed intent on stopping us from pursuing this goal. Instead, we fostered new friends who'd support us. True friends will support you no matter what you choose to do. We hadn't even considered that we would be too old to be parents. We were going to have these kids despite what anyone thought, did or said, and our plan was to remain physically and mentally young and positive. This meant we'd play sports, stay slim, monitor our health and diet so we would be able to participate in life with our new kids. Remember, if someone hasn't been down the track you want to go along, they can't give advice on what you should do. All they can do is put their own attitudes and limitations on you.

What the statistics said

The success rate for our goal was only 31 per cent for women under 35, plunging to around 4 per cent for women aged 42, and the statistics indicated that Barb could only expect to produce low-quality eggs. Combine this with my lack of sperm and the chances of conception were less than 2 per cent.

Second, they said that Barb's chances of carrying a baby for the full term at her age were also low. There would be increased odds of deformities, stillbirths and genetic abnormalities and Down's Syndrome. If ever there was a goal that had everything and everyone against it, this was it. But the worst thing that could happen was that we would adopt, and that was still an excellent Plan B.

Next, I underwent a series of testicular operations to establish if I had any viable sperm. My tests came out negative – my sperm was unviable because the radiation I had received for cancer had destroyed it. *'Forget it – buy a dog,'* said one urologist. So we fired him, took time off to recover and went back to searching the Internet. We decided that we would now be in control of this project and we'd become the experts to decide our own path. When 'experts' or other well-intentioned people tell you that something can't be done, find new experts and new friends who believe in you and what you want to achieve. You see, if we'd listened to the advice of the experts when I was first diagnosed with cancer, I'd probably have been dead a long time by now.

Don't take advice from people who have never done what you want to do.

Round 2

A sperm is simply a courier for a man's DNA so we decided to harvest my immobile sperm anyway, insert it into Barb's eggs via IVF, and hope that there was some DNA present to cause conception. So I put my balls back on the chopping block and the date was set for the extraction. Barb underwent a hormone injection program for 26 days to hopefully produce enough eggs for the numbers game to work its magic.

The date was set for my DNA transfer into Barb's eggs and the implanting of the successful embryos – the doctors were amazed that she had produced 27 'fair-quality' eggs. These eggs all received my DNA from the collected sperm and all fertilized. Holy football team, Batman! We'll have our own childcare centre soon! We monitored these embryos for the next five days to see how many would survive and be ready for implantation.

On day six, the doctor summoned an enthusiastic Allan and Barbara to his office and announced that all the embryos had failed. None had succeeded. We had lost the lot.

We were crushed. Barb was unable to speak for days. She was in shock and upset that the technique had completely failed. Over the next few weeks, we started to talk about it and decided to try again in another six months when our bodies had recovered. It meant that I would once again put what was left of my balls on the block for this goal and Barb would again take the course of hormone injections.

The doctors advised us not to proceed again as it would be even harder for us this time and we would both be nearly a year older. We calmly told the doctors that if they wouldn't help us, we'd find someone who would. Back to the Internet.

If your 'advisors' don't believe you can achieve your goals, get new advisors. It's your goal, not theirs. They are just advisors with an opinion.

Round 3

We focused on the end goal and not on our current failure, which kept us motivated. We heard about a doctor in Beijing who had perfected a technique of artificially inseminating female pigs by extracting the DNA code directly from male pigs. Sydney IVF had recently brought him to Australia so he could test this technique on humans. This new technique involved hunting for the DNA source and not the sperm. It would be collected and then inserted directly into female eggs, just as the doctor and his team had successfully done with pigs.

Sydney IVF accepted us into the program but warned that our odds of success were very low because of Barb's age and my radiation treatment. I would now undergo another operation to track down and extract my DNA. This kind of operation makes most people go pale and feel ill when they hear the details. They removed my right testicle and, while it was still attached to my body, put it on a plate. Then they pulled it apart like an orange, flattening it out like a pizza with a type of hammer, and, using a special microscope worn on the doctor's head, they searched for the DNA source.

I would be unconscious on the operating table. The surgeon would have my balls in one hand and a mallet in the other – any man's nightmare!

At the end of this procedure, they would roll what was left of my right testicle into a ball shape – just as you'd roll putty between your palms – wrap medical tape around it, reinsert it into me and sew everything back up. The downside of this operation was that I could suffer a haemorrhage (which I did!) and walk like John Wayne for the next six months (which I did!). The upside was that my voice could become higher-pitched and I could sing Beach Boys harmonies!

Finally, I could audition for The Vienna Boys' Choir.

Over six weeks, Barb had daily hormone injections to increase her egg production and to be ready for my DNA transfer on the right day. I had become competent at delivering injections during my cancer therapy so I volunteered to administer her daily injections. The whole experience was physically tough for us both, but there is a price to pay for every worthwhile goal you want to achieve.

Barb became even more steely in her resolve to make it work from her side. She began talking to her eggs and giving them instructions. She told them what they had to do, and would tell them what she was doing – whether she was cooking, jogging or working. While visualisation is a vital part of goal achievement, I began to worry about her mental health and was afraid she could suffer a collapse if the procedure failed again. But Barb was convinced that it would work, and so she happily had in-depth conversations with her ovaries every day. She also began to wear baby bibs to her medical appointments and around the house. She was faithfully following the principle that you must have complete belief in yourself and never consider any outcome other than what you want. Your brain has three billion cells that instruct your body what to do. I had successfully used this same principle to beat cancer so why couldn't Barb tell her body exactly what she wanted it to do?

I proceeded with my third testicular operation – right ball on the block this time and doctor with mallet in hand. Once again my DNA was collected and my voice pitch went even higher. You see, the higher a man's testosterone, the deeper his voice becomes. That's why baritones have twice as many orgasms as sopranos. The positive side of this surgery was that I could now sing Frankie Valli songs. But I'll never sing 'Duke of Earl' again.

Our mid-air experience

I was delivering Barb's next course of hormones via a giant needle thrust daily into her thigh for the next 26 days. The final injection with IVF is called the 'trigger injection' and it instructs the ovaries to release the eggs for collection. It must be given at an exact time within a ten-minute time window. On the day of the 'trigger injection' we were flying to Sydney – a one-hour flight – and I had to deliver the injection within 30 minutes of our arrival at Sydney airport.

Unfortunately, due to air traffic congestion, the plane's departure was 20 minutes late. We sat on the tarmac counting down the time with the trigger injection ready in a chiller bag at my feet. Finally we were approaching Sydney airport when the captain announced that due to congestion, we would remain in a holding pattern for another 30 minutes in turbulent weather. I would need to give Barb the trigger injection on the descent or the entire IVF cycle would be lost!

I urgently explained the situation to the cabin staff, who said that we were not permitted to remove our seatbelts or go to the bathroom for the needle delivery as we had planned. I said that if we couldn't use the bathroom then I would inject her right there in the seat and this could terrify the other, already nervous passengers. The cabin staff insisted that the injection wasn't going to happen but I explained that it would, whether they liked it or not – and I produced the needle.

I thought, *What's the worst that could happen?* I might be arrested on arrival for disobeying the flight crew. But so what? I'd meet new and interesting people in jail.

I consulted the captain, who agreed that we could use the curtained-off kitchen area for the injection. As we unbuckled our seatbelts and moved forward, the plane hit air turbulence and began to bounce around. In the kitchen, Barb pulled up her dress and lowered her knickers as I readied the needle while trying to keep my balance as the plane was bounced around like a balloon. I hit her hard and fast and sunk the needle up to the hilt. She yelped and burst into even more tears – but I was jubilant! The job was done!

Follow through with your plan of action despite what others may say, think or do.

Personally, I thought I would be able to handle the IVF procedure like a logical science project, but it didn't happen that way. It's an emotional experience that no-one can really be prepared for when they begin the process. If you are serious about achieving your goal – whatever it may be – you must resolve to do what is necessary, especially when the going gets tough.

Two days later Barb produced another 25 eggs and I underwent another round of testicular surgery to obtain fresh DNA, which was implanted into her eggs. This time we were rewarded with three healthy embryos – two male, one female. Two male embryos were implanted and the girl was placed into cryo-suspension for future use.

It is overwhelming to witness the insertion of a live embryo into the womb. I watched the procedure on a monitor. It is very spiritual stuff. As we walked out of the clinic an hour later, Barb looked at me calmly and said, *'I'm pregnant.'* I comforted and supported her, but at the same time I didn't want to overplay the situation because the chances of success were statistically remote. It was almost impossible for us even to have arrived at this point. I didn't want Barb to be traumatised if it all failed which, statistically speaking, it probably would.

The doctors explained that the hormone injections, my testicular surgeries and our previous medical failures had, in fact, been the easy part. Barb would now have to carry this embryo for at least 12 weeks before the pregnancy could be considered viable. And at nearly 43 years of age her chances were slim, they reiterated. That night, I searched the Internet for adoption agencies and for the type of dog we could buy. It's not that I didn't have faith; I have always considered the statistical probabilities of any venture and would have a back-up plan ready. I know that you must have faith in your ability to get what you want despite the odds, but now Barb was thinking her way into pregnancy and instructing her body cells what to do. I had never heard of anyone doing this. It was a mind-stretching concept, and yet it was the same process I had used to beat cancer. I'd had absolute faith that I would survive cancer, and I was now watching Barb using this process to produce new life.

Observing Barb do this with pregnancy gave me a feeling of awe. It was like watching Roger Bannister run the four-minute mile. I didn't tell her what I was feeling at the time because I wanted her to succeed and I had read

Authors ride rollercoaster of IVF

AS I sat listening to famous authors/counsellors/body language experts Barbara and Allan Pease's experience with IVF, I felt torn between a number of emotions.

I was swept up in their excitement at finally conceiving after 13 years together. I shared their anticipation about the upcoming birth of their baby boy (Barb was eight-and-a-half months pregnant when we talked). Still, I was horrified by the incredibly emotional experience they had been through.

"Despite counselling so many couples over the years, and really being in touch with how the human brain works and how couples relate to each other, we had no idea going through the IVF process would be such a rollercoaster ride," Allan said. The

couple already had four children over 21 from previous marriages.

"We really wanted a child together but because we had other children, and because I'm such a research junkie and found out all about the scientific side of the process before we actually went ahead with it, I honestly went into it thinking the result wouldn't really bother me either way," Allan said. "I thought we would both deal with whatever happened brilliantly. We knew all about human behaviour and assumed it would be a simple process but once we were in the middle of it all, there was no controlling the situation and we just had to let the emotions roll."

to page 6

Allan and Barbara Pease relax at home before the birth of their son with older children Jasmine and Adam.

about other women who had successfully followed this path. Now I was living with one. As her husband, I remained silently nervous while she was steely and resolute, eerily calm and confident that we would have at least one child – maybe two – on the way. Barb continued to talk to her embryos, she sang songs to them, explained everything she was doing in detail, wore baby clothes around her neck, read stories to them and continued decorating a baby's room.

Brandon was born on 8 March 2005 after a 12-hour, drug-free labour.

Brandon Pease – six days old.

Pair humbled by surreal experience

from page 4

Barbara agreed the process was the most emotional experience she had ever had, and probably would ever have: "The whole thing was such a surreal experience. When you fall pregnant the natural way, it just sort of happens but with IVF, you actually get to watch your follicles grow and you measure them, you see the cells divide and it is literally like watching life being created.

"We went through two cycles of IVF and the first was absolutely devastating for me because we lost every follicle — it was like losing my children and I felt like I was mourning a death. You've got to remember that for weeks previously you're being injected with hormones, so you're unstable as it is and then to realise all of your follicles had died and the whole crazy process had failed was just heartbreaking.

"I cried for days and days and nothing could console me. It was so hard for Allan because he had never seen me in such a state and there was just nothing he could do to make it better. It was so hard on both of us."

Barbara said the second time around she was slightly more composed: "I knew what I was getting myself into the second time around.

"I was so worried the second cycle would fail as well but somehow I just felt it was going to work. When I found out I was pregnant I was so relieved and so happy, but there were still more hurdles to jump because I was older and there was a good chance I'd lose it. But I didn't and all the daily injections, the emotions and the pain were well worth it.

"I feel like I was meant to go through all of this so I would be able to understand other women in the same position. Without actually experiencing it I would never have had any idea just how intense it could be. And it has actually worked out wonderfully because Allan's daughter Jasmine, who is 23, will be giving birth to her first child only eight weeks after I do — she fell pregnant naturally and it's going to be so wonderful to welcome both our first child and our first grandchild into the world at the same time."

Barbara and Allan's story has the best kind of ending. Not only will the couple's first baby together be due around the time you are reading this article, one of their other eggs from the second cycle was successfully fertilised too and is now frozen in Nambour Selangor Hospital's IVF clinic, waiting to be implanted in a year or so's time. "It's a little girl and the fraternal twin of the boy we are about to have. When it came to the crunch and we had to decide what to do with the fertilised egg, we just couldn't not have it," Allan said. ∎

Barb's personal perspective

Brandon was born when I was almost 43. Even though my pregnancy and his birth were difficult roads to travel and were filled with poor statistics, I made the decision not to take on board the negative talk I was given by many of the doctors, relatives and others. I made the decision to be positive about the outcome I wanted, to become pregnant and have a drug-free delivery. I never thought that I could not do this and I only ever visualised the outcomes I wanted.

Most of our friends couldn't believe that I would give up my life of fame, excitement and travelling the world to go back to changing nappies and breast-feeding again. But I was convinced that going to school carnivals and making my kid's lunches were what I truly wanted to do now. I couldn't imagine it not being true. After holding Brandon, it became true, just as I had pictured it. From a total of 57 eggs that I had produced during the IVF treatments, I now held my baby in my arms. It was a feeling I will never forget.

Two amazing and blissful years after Brandon's birth, I told Allan I really wanted to have a daughter too. My daughter was genetically perfect and in cryo-suspension, and I couldn't get her out of my mind because I'd always wanted a daughter. Allan was nervous at first because we now had five children and the odds of conceiving again were even lower than the first time. I was now 46; the doctors said I could risk the baby's health and my own life. But I positively, definitely, absolutely, unquestionably wanted a daughter. I didn't believe that I couldn't do it all again, despite the poor odds.

As I lay in bed night after night picturing how this could happen, it soon became clear to me that I could do it again.

My body was saying, 'Yes, you can.' The doctors were steadfast in their opinions that this was a dangerous road to travel, fraught with even bigger risks than last time, even if the process of unfreezing the embryo was successful. Friends and family were aghast and tried to 'talk sense into me'. I again made the concrete decision that I would and could do it again, despite the statistics and negative odds. If only a tiny percentage of women could succeed at this, I'd be one of them. I also decided to only be around people who believed this was possible and who would support me.

My little girl embryo – I had named her Bella – was successfully unfrozen and implanted in me. I spoke to her non-stop and told her what to do – to attach herself to my womb, to be positive, and that I would meet her soon. I visualised every cell in my body and gave them all clear instructions. To everyone's amazement, Bella attached herself to my womb, and I passed all the critical early pregnancy tests for an older woman. Nine months later, Bella became Brandon's fraternal twin sister – born three years after him. I chose a natural birth again...not bad for a 'geriatric' woman!

I am often asked what it is like having a second family as an older woman. It's the best! I shared both pregnancies with my stepdaughters, Melissa and Jasmine, who were both pregnant at the same time as me. What an experience to have my 26-year-old son Adam watch me carry his brother and sister, and for him to hold each of them just after they were born. It was just mind-blowing. I am now 54 and Allan is 65 and our new children keep us young. Most people our age are in the empty-nest stage of life and spend a lot of time eating, drinking, golfing and travelling. Instead, Allan and I chase two young children around the house, attend school every day, go to sports events, play tennis, practise martial arts, and exercise with Brandon and Bella. Our social circle consists of people in their twenties and thirties.

Allan and I are surrounded by lots of little people – and we love it. Brandon and Bella are uncle and aunty to eight kids their own age, who are also part of our new family. I'd never change any part of how it all happened. When anyone tells you there's only a small chance you can achieve something, remember that it's only their opinion based on their experiences. Or they may be projecting their own inadequacies onto you. It doesn't mean that you can't achieve it. Usually it means you need to take a positive attitude, work at it harder and decide to be in the minority of those who succeed. That's what I did. I decided that someone had to be in that small successful group, so why couldn't it be me?

And I really didn't want another dog.

Left: Barb's visual image of Bella and Bella herself.

Positive affirmations

A year before Bella was conceived, at an English market Barbara saw a 19th-century painting of a blonde girl who resembled the daughter she had pictured in her mind. My father Ray bought it for her as a present. Barb hung it on the wall for six months before she attempted to become pregnant with Bella. Some people thought Barb had lost the plot with this but she used it as a visual image of what she intended to create. You can compare the picture Ray purchased at that market with the photo of Bella.

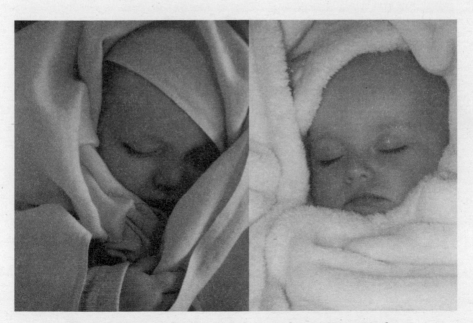

Brandon and Bella, both aged seven months. This is how they would have looked if they had been born at the same time.

In the media

The media, especially women's magazines, were keen on our story and it began to appear everywhere, including two segments on *60 Minutes*. We received a flood of calls and emails from other couples who had either given up hope of having kids or who had been told to forget it. Here is one letter Barb received from complete strangers, Helen and Jamie.

Sometimes in life, a spur-of-the moment decision can have the most dramatic impact on your life. For me it was choosing to send an email to a stranger I had read about in a magazine. One simple sentence from a person I'd never met helped turn my fading optimism around and give me the strength to keep on going. Our dream to have a family proved to be one of the most challenging experiences of our lives.

Our story is one that many couples all over the world are experiencing. Yes, we were another older couple trying to have children. After three heartbreaking miscarriages and close to a year of grieving we finally took the bull by the horns and decided to explore the IVF program.

Friends who had also struggled to have kids and who had watched us go through our ups and downs were persistent with trying to get us to go through IVF, but it wasn't so easy for me to persuade my husband, as he believed IVF was for couples who couldn't conceive. It took me a year to convince him to have a consultation and the response from the doctor was both confronting and overwhelming. He said that there was no time to wait and we should have looked into getting help earlier! Hey…I didn't meet my husband until I was 33!

I was also very concerned about carrying a baby after miscarrying so many times. It's a full-on clinical experience, going off the pill, injecting yourself every day, going into hospital to get your eggs collected and Jamie going in to 'shake his tail feather'. After the first round my egg count was low and I could see the doctor's concern. He asked if I would consider using a donor egg and did I have any sisters? I was devastated. He actually asked me these things while he was implanting the one good egg we harvested from the first cycle, so instead of feeling positive and excited about getting implanted I came out in tears and called my younger sister. I was in shock with what he had told me and the waiting game on my one egg was painful. Unfortunately, it didn't hold.

I believe that being told I might have to consider donor eggs while I was getting implanted had a lot to do with the first egg not working because my expectation level was low.

I started researching everything I could about IVF and stumbled across a story in a magazine about a couple who had defied the odds and had produced twins born three years apart. The couple were Barb and Allan Pease. So in a spur-of-the-moment decision I searched for them on the Internet, found their website and emailed my enquiries, not really expecting an answer. The same day I received this email back from Barbara:

Thank you for getting in contact with us and I wish you all the best…but also remember…don't believe anyone who says it's impossible – just believe in yourself and know that it will happen.

   Knowing what I know now…I believe that I have my twins because of my belief in me…My doctor's number is XXXXXXX. I'm not sure where you are but once you are pregnant your GP can take over.

Thinking of you
Barb Pease

Two sentences stuck in my mind:
'Don't believe anyone…just believe in yourself and know that it will happen…'
'Knowing what I know now…I believe that I have my twins because of my belief in me…'

I printed Barb and Allan's story and clipped it to our fridge. I must have read it 100 times! We decided to stick with it, whatever happened. After two more long and tortuous failed attempts, we again regrouped. This time Jamie and I made the decision that we were just going to keep trying long-term and get on with our lives, book holidays and enjoy each other. Our third try, they implanted two eggs.

It was at this point Jamie and I did the silliest things to keep our positivity up. It's what Barb and Allan called 'visualisation'. We painted two chicken eggs — one as a little boy and one as a little girl. We call them our 'Happy Eggs' and put them on our kitchen bench. Every morning and evening when we were making breakfast or dinner we would look at our 'Happy Eggs' and smile and talk to them. We both become very attached to them and they made us smile every day. Barb had also told me to see the humorous side of everything because it would increase my odds of success.

I emailed Barb about our 'Happy Eggs', feeling a little silly but I thought she might like our silliness. Barb emailed back with a story about what she did every time she went to the doctor. She would wear a baby's bib — alternating between one pink and one blue. The doctor thought she was nuts, but it made me laugh and there is something about keeping light-hearted and happy during this process that felt really good.

Well, the waiting game for us finally came to an end. I went in for a blood test and it confirmed I was pregnant. YAY! We were so excited. I was still very nervous due to my pregnancy history and knew it would be a long road before I felt totally comfortable being pregnant. We went in for a scan and found that only one egg had taken. But we were still so excited to know that we had one 'Happy Egg' growing inside me.

The pregnancy was not easy after that, and I had many issues to contend with. But what had changed was my attitude. I had an inner belief that it would all be okay and every time I got hit with another medical issue, I would talk to my egg and tell him to hang in there and let him know how much we loved him.

Our egg is now our new son. Jamie and I feel like the luckiest people in the world!

Our persistence and bonding through the most difficult years cemented our love for each other in a way that may never have happened had we given up early. My shift in attitude was truly the biggest difference. Our family and friends were amazing sources of strength and Barb Pease helped me to believe in myself at a truly vulnerable time in our lives. We will be forever grateful.

What if we were wrong?

So, what if we went through all these procedures and weren't successful? What if it had all failed? Statistically speaking, our odds were small. But other people had achieved it and more will be successful in the future, so we proceeded with hardened determination. We were going to have kids and raise them despite everything, and Barb's pregnancy path was the ultimate way to go. Worst-case scenario, we'd adopt and that would still be wonderful. We decided that whatever the outcome was to be, we would be happy with it. Even if our first plan didn't work out, we would achieve our goal somehow, no matter what.

Many people are reluctant to take a positive path because sometimes the odds look overwhelming. Even when the odds are against you, if you want to achieve something it doesn't mean you shouldn't do it. When you decide to take a path toward a goal that you really want, new doors will open. You will see other options and possibilities that you wouldn't have seen or considered if you had not set off down that track.

When you program clearly defined goals into your RAS, it will search for a way to give you what you want.

Chapter 16

Putting it all Together

Let's summarise the key points in *The Answer*.

Success in life and achieving the things you want, or becoming who you want to be, are more a matter of planning and organisation than of talent. We all know very talented people who go nowhere, and others who don't seem to have a lot going for them but who blaze trails. Most people don't achieve as much with their lives as they could because they think about **how** they could achieve something instead of deciding **what** they really want. As you now know, deciding what is the most critical step to success. And, as you would have discovered by now, when you decide the **what**, the **hows** will appear around you. Build these into your plan of action and set achievable deadlines.

The Answer has explained why so many of the things you may already be familiar with, work – visualisation, affirmations, goal-setting, deadlines, prayers, 'The Universe', the Law of Attraction, and so on. You now have the science to prove how and why they all work. It's about how you program your RAS with your self-talk and your expectations.

The exciting breakthrough in *The Answer* is that you can deliberately program your RAS by choosing the exact messages you send to it from your conscious mind. If your expectations are positive, you automatically program your RAS to seek information about positive behaviours and screen out information about negative behaviours.

This means you can create your own reality. Nothing in this book is connected to willpower – it all happens in this small bunch of neural fibres running through your brain stem – your Reticular Activating System – your RAS.

Write it down

The most successful people in life write down their thoughts and prioritise their ideas. As soon as their thoughts are on paper, the RAS begins to source the answers to achieving what they want. Keep writing your lists of anything in life you find interesting or exciting and don't judge them – just write them down. This focuses your attention on what really matters and gets your RAS aroused and working in your favour. Your RAS will always locate the exact steps needed to get there.

Keep adding to your list and be sure that what you set as goals are the things you really want and not what others expect of you. Write and rewrite your lists. Discover what your passions are and remove money from the equation so that you can think clearly without worrying about finances. And make plans to move toward 80/20 lifestyle activities.

Break it down and set deadlines

Break your goals down into bite-sized pieces and eat one piece at a time. If you don't look like you are able to reach an important deadline, adjust it. The difference between successful people and the rest is that successful people are action-oriented. They might not look very graceful when they begin, but they are moving forward. And they stay on track despite other people's attempts to dislodge them. You can put a deadline on anything, including negative thinking.

Take responsibility

Everything you will have in your life will be based on the choices you make. It's not your parents, your past relation-ships, your job, the economy, the weather, your race or your age that are to blame. You, and only you, are responsible for every decision and choice you make. The great news is that you have 100 per cent control over your choices from now on. In *The Answer* you have learned how to live a 'want to' life, not a 'have to' life. From today, decide to take 100 per cent responsibility for everything in your life. If you catch yourself complaining about anything, stop immediately. Decide right now to make changes in your responses to the events in your life. Begin talking positively about what you can do and will do.

Use affirmations and visualisation

There are countless stories of people who have achieved their goals by using affirmations to focus their mind on their intended outcomes and who visualise their success ahead of time. Goals must be *mind-accomplished* before they can become materially accomplished, and no-one can rise above their self-imposed limitations. From today, every time you say something negative, restate it in a positive way. Visualisation works because it strengthens the neural pathways in your brain for any particular skill, and it will work for almost any goal you can set. From today, only visualise the things you do want, not the ones you don't. Visualisation and affirmations can break down the barriers to your success and set you free to unlock more creativity and untapped potential than you ever dreamed possible. Use visualisation and affirmations to keep your enthusiasm high and to give you the time necessary to develop the new habits you need.

All successful athletes practise their sport both physically and mentally. Always see yourself winning. What you tell yourself will happen. Continually practise *positive* actions until they become 'can do' habits.

Your life is the sum total of your past affirmations. When you practise affirmations, the Law of Reinforcement begins to work for you. First, we seek out those strengths and changes we have stated and begin to see in the real world the things we expect to see, just like Darrin did with his spinning back-kick, as Scott did with Dilbert and Sam did with his short life. We begin to act like the person we have resolved to be.

Never think about what you *don't* want to happen. Only think about what you do want, regardless of the outcome of a situation. What you think about and what you affirm is what you'll usually get.

Form new habits
Intentionally acquiring the habits of successful people will lead you to the success you want. Holding on to non-productive habits is a millstone around your neck and prevents you from moving forward. Your eventual success – or not – in any venture will be controlled by your learned, habitual thoughts and attitudes. Run your business life by a diary and keep it with you at all times. Buy a book on how to remember people's names. If you smoke, drink or take drugs, take the necessary steps to quit now.

Follow through, despite what anyone says, thinks or does
Well-meaning friends, relatives or others may try to stop you from moving toward your goals because they either love you, loathe you or don't want to look bad themselves. When you set your goal and create a plan with a deadline, take that first step – despite what others may think,

say or do. The only way to avoid criticism is to do nothing, say nothing and be nothing.

Give yourself permission to walk away from anything that gives you bad vibes. You don't need to explain it to anybody, just trust your inner voice. Acknowledge today that you have been responsible for attracting into your life the things and people that now surround you. If you are not thrilled by the lifestyle and achievements of your five closest friends, find new ones. If you stay only with your current group of friends you can only expect to continue to achieve the average of that group. If you don't want to be the average of your current friends, find new ones. Develop an agreeable nature and make others feel right, whatever their opinion. Acknowledge that it's all right for them to think that way while, at the same time, restating what you believe to be true.

Accept fear and worry as normal

If you're stressed, worried or depressed about any of the things in your life and your negative thoughts have become a habit, put a deadline on when you will get over them. Decide that from a specific time on a specific day, you will not think negatively about the things that happened to you in the past. Disasters happen to us all; they are a part of life. But just because you get knocked down doesn't mean you're out of the game. You are only defeated if you stay down. Decide in advance that when tragedy strikes, you'll pull yourself out of it. Expect that you may feel fearful when new or unexpected opportunities arise, but don't let this stop you from working to achieve your goal.

Play the numbers

Remind yourself that everything you set as a goal will be based on number sequences and formulas. Every venture in life has a set of statistics – a ratio – attached to it. You also have a personal set of statistics that will determine your odds of success. Record all your daily activities, such as how many times you attempted something, how often you succeeded or failed, what achieved a result and what did not, and soon your ratios will appear.

Reclaim your life

Don't take any path that someone tries to push you down, regardless of how honourable this person's intentions may seem. Take charge of your own life, reclaim yourself and choose to become the person you want to be. If you are not working every day on something that excites you, plan to get out of it. Most people don't like what they do for a living. Too many people claim they are too busy earning a living to be able to do what they really want to do. Don't be one of them.

Don't give up

The beginning is always the hardest part. If you feel like quitting, reread your goal list and think only about what you want as your outcome. Go as far as you can see, and when you get there you'll be able to see further than you could at the start. Stick with your goals despite what anyone may say, think or do. Today it is possible to have anything you want in life provided you can first think of it, then write it down on a prioritised list, and follow the rules and principles we have given in this book.

Finally…

The RAS is such a powerful tool that it can take you anywhere you want to go. It's your personal GPS. All you need to do is to first decide what goals you'd like to achieve and write them down and create deadlines for the **A** list items. When the **hows** begin to appear around you, develop them into a plan. Then move forward despite what others may think, say or do. Learn the new habits you'll need to make your journey easier, develop positive affirmations, and use visualisation. And whatever happens along the way, see the humorous side of things. That's what Barb and I have always done because we know it works. And it will work for you when you decide to use it.

Take what you do in life seriously but never take yourself too seriously. Make an agreement with yourself that you'll look for the humorous side of anything that happens along the way. The best day of your life is the one on which you decide that your life is your own – no excuses or apologies, no-one to lean on, to rely on or to blame. This is the day your life really begins.

And here is the quote with which we started this book:

'Whatever the mind can conceive and believe, the body can achieve.'
Napoleon Hill, 1937

References

Chapter 1

Burlet, S., Tyler, C. J. & Leonard, C. S. (2002). 'Direct and indirect excitation of laterodorsal tegmental neurons by hypocretin/orexin peptides: Implications for wakefulness and narcolepsy'. *Journal of Neuroscience* 22 (7): 2862–2872. PMID 11923451.

Evans, B. M. (2003). 'Sleep, consciousness and the spontaneous and evoked electrical activity of the brain. Is there a cortical integrating mechanism?'. Neuophysiologie clinique 33: 1–10. "https://en.wikipedia.org/wiki/Digital_object_identifier" "https://dx.doi.org/10.1016%2Fs0987-7053%2803%2900002-9" 10.1016/s0987-7053(03)00002-9.

Garcia-Rill, E. (1997). 'Disorders of the reticular activating system'. *Medical Hypotheses* 49 (5): 379–387. doi:10.1016/S0306-9877(97) 90083-9. PMID 9421802.

Garcia-Rill, E. (2008). 'Long-term deficits of preterm birth: Evidence for arousal and attentional disturbances'. *Clinical Neurophysiology* 119 (6): 1281–1291. doi:10.1016/j.clinph.2007.12.021. PMC 2670248. PMID 18372212.

Garcia-Rill, E., Buchanan, R., McKeon, K., Skinner, R. R. & Wallace, T. (2007). 'Smoking during pregnancy: Postnatal effects on arousal and attentional brain systems'. *NeuroToxicology* 28 (5): 915–923. doi:10.1016/j.neuro.2007.01.007. PMC 3320145. PMID 17368773.

Garcia-Rill, E., Heister, D. S., Ye, M., Charlesworth, A. & Hayar, A. (2007). 'Electrical coupling: novel mechanism for sleep-wake control'. *Sleep* 30 (11): 1405–1414. PMC 2082101. PMID 18041475.

Kinomura, S., Larsson, J., Gulyas, B. & Roland, P. E. (1996). 'Activation by attention of the human reticular formation and

thalamic intralaminar nuclei'. *Science* 271 (5248): 512–515.
doi:10.1126/science.271.5248.512. PMID 8560267.

Kumar, V. M., Mallick, B. N., Chhina, G. S. & Singh, B. (1984).
'Influence of ascending reticular activating system on preoptic
neuronal-activity'. *Experimental Neurology* 86 (1): 40–52.
doi:10.1016/0014 -4886(84)90065-7. PMID 6479280.

Magoun, H. W. (1952). 'An ascending reticular activating system
in the brain stem'. *Ama Archives of Neurology and Psychiatry* 67
(2): 145–154. doi: 10.1001/archneurpsyc.1952.02320140013002.
PMID 14893989.

Reiner, P. B. (1995). 'Are mesopontine cholinergic neurons either
necessary or sufficient components of the ascending reticular
activating system?'. *Seminars in the Neurosciences* 7 (5): 355–
359. doi:10.1006 /smns.1995.0038.

Robinson, D. (1999). 'The technical, neurological and
psychological significance of "alpha", "delta" and "theta" waves
confounded in EEG evoked potentials: a study of peak latencies'.
Clinical Neurophysiology 110 (8): 1427–1434. doi:10.1016/
S1388-2457(99)00078-4. PMID 10454278.

Rothballer, A. B. (1956). 'Studies on the adrenaline-
sensitive component of the reticular activating system'.
Electroencephalography and Clinical Neurophysiology 8 (4):
603–621. doi:10.1016/0013-4694(56)90084-0. PMID 13375499.

Ruth, R. E. & Rosenfeld, J. P. (1977). 'Tonic reticular activating
system – relationship to aversive brain-stimulation effects'.
Experimental Neurology 57 (1): 41–56. doi:10.1016/0014-
4886(77)90043-7. PMID 196879.

Shute, C. C. D. & Lewis, P. R. (1967). 'The ascending cholinergic
reticular system: neocortical, olfactory and subcortical
projections'. *Brain* 90 (3): 497–520. doi:10.1093/brain/90.3.497.
PMID 6058140.

Steriade, M. (1995). 'Neuromodulatory systems of thalamus
and neocortex'. *Seminars in the Neurosciences* 7 (5): 361–370.
doi:10.1006 /smns.1995.0039.

Steriade, M. (1996). 'Arousal: Revisiting the reticular activating
system'. *Science* 272 (5259): 225–226. doi:10.1126/
science.272.5259.225. PMID 8602506.248

Svorad, D. (1957). 'Reticular activating system of brain stem and

animal hypnosis'. *Science* 125 (3239): 156–156. doi:10.1126/
science.125.3239.156. PMID 13390978.

Vincent, S. R. (2000). 'The ascending reticular activating
system – from aminergic neurons to nitric oxide'. *Journal of
Chemical Neuroanatomy* 18 (1–2): 23–30. doi:10.1016/S0891-
0618(99)00048-4. PMID 10708916.

http://sleepdisorders.sleepfoundation.org/chapter-1-normal-sleep/
neurobiology-of-sleep/

http://www.ncbi.nlm.nih.gov/pmc/articles/PMC2701283/

Chapter 2

http://www.dominican.edu/academics/ahss/undergraduate-programs/
psych/faculty/assets-gail-matthews/researchsummary2.pdf

https://www.washingtonpost.com/news/on-leadership/
wp/2013/10/10/only-13-percent-of-people-worldwide-actually-
like-going-to-work/

Chapter 3

Hill, P. L. & Turiano, N. A. (2014). 'Purpose in life as a predictor
of mortality across adulthood'. *Psychological Science*. doi:
10.1177/0956797614531799.

Shackell, Erin M. & Standing, Lionel G. 'Mind over matter:
Mental training increases physical strength'. *North American
Journal of Psychology* 9: 189–200.

http://www.medicalnewstoday.com/articles/276893.php

Chapter 6

Brayand, F. & Moller, B. (2006). 'Predicting the future burden of
cancer'. *Nature Reviews Cancer* 6: 63–74. doi:10.1038/nrc1781.

Calle, E. E., Rodriguez, C., Walker-Thurmond, K. & Thun,
M. J. (2003). 'Overweight, obesity, and mortality from
cancer in a prospectively studied cohort of U.S. adults'. *New
England Journal of Medicine* 348: 1625–1638. doi: 10.1056/
NEJMoa021423.

Doll, R. & Peto, R. (1981). 'The causes of cancer: quantitative
estimates of avoidable risks of cancer in the United States today'.
Journal of the National Cancer Institute 66: 191–308.

Kolonel, L. N., Altshuler, D. & Henderson, B. E. (2004). 'The

multiethnic cohort study: exploring genes, lifestyle and cancer risk'. *Nature Reviews Cancer* 4: 519–27. doi:10.1038/nrc1389.
http://www.who.int/mediacentre/news/releases/2003/pr27/en/
https://www.apf.asn.au/Members/Information/A-Skydiver-s-Guide-to-Mental-Training/default.aspx
https://students.education.unimelb.edu.au/LiteracyResearch/pub/Projects/AKurzman.pdf
http://www.psych.nyu.edu/oettingen/Barry%20Kappes,%20H.,%20&%20Oettingen,%20G.%20(2011).%20JESP.pdf

Chapter 7

Ahsen, A. (1984). 'ISM: The triple code model for imagery and psychophysiology'. *Journal of Mental Imagery* 8 (4): 15–42.

Behncke, L. (2004). 'Mental skills training for sports: A brief review'. *Athletic Insight. The Online Journal of Sport Psychology.* [www.athleticInsight.com/html]. Retrieved 22 April 2010.

Bell, R., Skinner, C. & Fisher, L. (2009). 'Decreasing putting yips in accomplished golfers via solution-focused guided imagery: A single-subject research design'. *Journal of Applied Sport Psychology* 21 (1): 1–14.

Boyd, J. & Munroe, K. (2003). 'The use of imagery in climbing'. Athletic Insight. *The Online Journal of Sport Psychology.* [www.athleticInsight.com/html]. Retrieved 21 March 2010.

Callow, N. & Hardy, L. (2001). 'Types of imagery associated with sport confidence in netball players of varying skills'. *Journal of Applied Sport Psychology* 13: 1–17.

Callow, N., Roberts, R. & Fawkes, J. (2006). 'Effects of dynamic and static imagery on vividness of imagery skiing performance, and confidence'. *Journal of Imagery Research in Sport and Physical Activity* 1: 1–15.

Calmels, C., Holmes, P., Berthoumieux, C. & Singer, R. (2004). 'The development of movement imagery vividness through a structured intervention in softball'. *Journal of Sport Behavior* 27: 307–322.

Cumming, J., Nordin, S., Horton, R. & Reynolds, S. (2006). 'Examining the direction of imagery and self-talk on dart-throwing performance and self-efficacy'. *The Sport Psychologist* 20: 257–274.

Driskell, J., Cooper, C. & Moran, A. (1994). 'Does mental practice enhance performance?' *Journal of Applied Sport Psychology* 79: 481–492.

Evans, L., Jones, L. & Mullen, R. (2004). 'An imagery intervention during the competitive season with an elite rugby union player'. *The Sport Psychologist* 18: 252–271.

Feltz, D. & Landers, D. (1983). 'The effects of mental practice on motor skill learning and performance: A meta-analysis'. *Journal of Sport Psychology* 5: 25–57.

Fischman, M. & Oxendine, J. (1993). 'Motor skill learning for effective coaching and performance'. In J. W. Williams (ed.), *Applied Sport Psychology* (Palo Alto, Calif.: Mayfield), pp. 11–23.

Glisky, M., Williams, J. & Kihlstrom, J. (1996). 'Internal and external imagery perspectives and performance on two tasks'. *Journal of Sport Behavior* 19 (1): 3–18.

Gould, D., Damarjian, N. & Greenleaf, C. (2002). 'Imagery training for peak performance'. In J. Van Raalte and B. Brewer (eds), *Exploring Sport and Exercise Psychology* (Washington, DC: American Psychological Association), 2nd edn, pp. 49–74.

Gray, S. (1990). 'Effect of visuo-motor rehearsal with videotaped modeling on racquet ball performance of beginning players'. *Perceptual and Motor Skills* 70: 379–385.

Green, L. (1993). 'The use of imagery in the rehabilitation of injured athletes'. In D. Pargman (ed.), *Psychological Bases of Sport Injuries* (Morgantown, WV: Fitness Information Technology), pp. 199–218.

Guillot, A. & Collet, C. (2008). 'Construction of the motor imagery integrative model in sport: A review and theoretical investigations of motor imagery use'. *International Review of Sport and Exercise Psychology* 1 (1): 31–44.

Guillot, A., Nadrowska, E. & Collet, C. (2009). 'Using motor imagery to learn tactical movements in basketball'. *Journal of Sport Behavior* 32 (2): 189–206.

Haanen, H., Hoenderdos, H., Van Romunde, L., Hop, W., Malle, C., Terwiel, J. & Hekster, G. B. (1991). 'Controlled trial of hypnotherapy in the treatment of refractory fibromyalgia'. *Journal of Rheumatology* 18: 72–75.

Hale, B. (1998). *Imagery Training: A Guide for Sports Coaches and Performers* (Leeds, UK: National Coaching Foundation).

Halgren, E., Dale, M., Sereno, R. & Tootell, R. (1999). 'Location of human face-selective cortex with respect to retinotopic areas'. *Human Brain Mapping* 7: 29–37.

Hall, C., Mack, D., Paivio, A. & Hausenblas, H. (1998). 'Imagery use by athletes: development of the Sport Imagery Questionnaire'. *International Journal of Sport Psychology* 29: 73–89.

Hall, C. & Pongrac, J. (1983). *Movement Imagery Questionnaire* (London, Ontario: University of Western Ontario).

Hall, E. & Erffemeyer, E. (1983). 'The effect of visuomotor behavior rehearsal with videotaped modeling on free throw accuracy of intercollegiate female basketball players'. *Journal of Sport Psychology* 5: 343–346.

Harris, D. & Robinson, W. (1986). 'The effect of skill level on EMG activity during internal and external imagery'. *Journal of Sport Psychology* 8: 105–111.

Hecker, J. & Kaczor, L. (1988). 'Application of imagery theory to sport psychology: Some preliminary findings'. *Journal of Sport and Exercise Psychology* 10: 363–373.

Holmes, P. & Collins, D. (2001). 'The PETTLEP approach to motor imagery. A functional equivalence model for sport psychologists.' *Journal of Applied Sport Psychology* 13: 60–83.

Isaac, A., Marks, D. & Russell, D. (1986). 'An instrument for assessing imagery of movement: The Vividness of Movement Imagery Questionnaire (VMIQ)'. *Journal of Mental Imagery* 10: 23–30.

Janssen, J. & Sheikh, A. (1994). 'Enhancing athletic performance through imagery: An overview'. In A. A. Sheikh & E. R. Korn (eds), *Imagery and Sport Physical Performance* (Amityville, NY: Bayood Publishing), pp. 1–22.

Jones, G. (1995). 'More than just a game: Research developments and issues in competitive anxiety in sport'. *British Journal of Psychology* 86: 449–478.

Klein, I., Paradis, A., Poline, J., Kosslyn, S. & LeBihan, D. (2000). 'Transient activity in human calcarine cortex during visual imagery'. *Journal of Cognitive Neuroscience* 12: 15–23.

Kosslyn, S., Ganis, G. & Thompson, W. (2001). 'Neural foundations of imagery'. *Nature Reviews Neuroscience* 2: 635–642.

Kosslyn, S., Thompson, W., Kim, I. & Alpert, N. (1995). 'Topographical representations of mental images in primary visual cortex'. *Nature* 3: 496–498.

Lambert, S. (1996). 'The effects of hypnosis/guided imagery on the postoperative course of children'. *Journal of Developmental and Behavioral Pediatrics* 17: 307–310.

Lang, P. (1979). 'A bioinformational theory of emotional imagery'. *Psychophysiology* 16: 495–512.

Lang. P., Kozak, M., Miller, G., Levin, D. & McLean, A. (1980). 'Emotional imagery: Conceptual structure and pattern of somato-visceral response'. *Psychophysiology* 17: 179–192.

Lang, P., Levin, D., Miller, G. & Kozak, M. (1983). 'Fear behavior, fear imagery, and the psychophysiology of emotion: The problem of affective response integration'. *Journal of Abnormal Psychology* 92: 276–306.

Lohr, B. & Scogin, F. (1998). 'Effects of self-administered visuo-motor behavioural rehearsal on sport performance of collegiate athletes'. *Journal of Sport Behaviour* 21 (2): 206–218.

MacKay, D. (1981). 'The problem of rehearsal or mental practice'. *Journal of Motor Behavior* 13: 274–285.

Mahoney, M., & Avener, M. (1977). Psychology of the elite athlete: an exploratory study. *Cognitive Therapy and Research* 1: 135–141.

Malone, M. & Strube, M. (1988). 'Meta-analysis of non-medical treatment for chronic pain'. Pain 34: 231–234.

Malouff, J., McGee, J., Halford, H. & Rooke, S. (2008). 'Effects of pre-competition positive imagery and self-instructions on accuracy of serving in tennis'. *Journal of Sport Behavior* 31 (3): 264–275.

Mamassis, G. & Doganis, G. (2004). 'Effects of a mental training program on juniors pre-competitive anxiety, self-confidence, and tennis performance'. *Journal of Applied Sport Psychology* 16: 118–137.

Marks, D. (1983). 'Mental imagery and consciousness: A theoretical review'. In A. Sheikh (ed.), *Imagery: Current Theory, Research, and Application* (New York: Wiley), pp. 96–130.

Martin, K. & Hall, C. (1995). 'Using mental imagery to enhance intrinsic motivation'. *Journal of Sport and Exercise Psychology* 17: 54–69.

Martin, K., Moritz, S. & Hall, C. (1999). 'Imagery use in sport: A literature review and applied model'. *The Sport Psychologist* 13: 245–268.

Mauer, M., Burnett, K., Oulette, E., Ironson, G. & Dandes, H. (1999). 'Medical hypnosis and orthopedic hand surgery: Pain perception, postoperative recovery, and therapeutic comfort'. *International Journal of Clinical and Experimental Hypnosis* 47: 144–161.

Moritz, S., Hall, C., Martin, K. & Vadocz, E. (1996). 'What are confident athletes imagining: An examination of image content'. *The Sport Psychologist* 10: 171–179.

Munroe, K., Giacobbi, P., Hall, C. & Weinberg, R. (2000). 'The four W's of imagery use: where, when, why, and what'. *The Sport Psychologist* 14: 119–137.

Munroe-Chandler, K. & Hall, C. (2007). 'Psychological interventions in sport'. In P. Crocker (ed.), *Introduction to Sport Psychology: A Canadian Perspective* (Toronto, ON: Pearson).

Murphy, S. & Jowdy, D. (1992). 'Imagery and mental practice'. In T. S. Horn (ed.), *Advances in Sport Psychology* (Champaign, IL: Human Kinetics), 2nd edn, pp. 221–250.

Murphy, S. & Martin, K. (2002). 'The use of imagery in sport'. In T. Horn (ed.), *Advances in Sport Psychology* (Champaign, IL: Human Kinetics), 2nd edn, pp. 405–439.

Nideffer, R. (1994). *Psyched to Win* (Champaign, IL: Human Kinetics).

Nideffer, R. & Sagal, M. (2006). 'Concentration and attention control training'. In J. M. Williams (ed.), *Applied Sport Psychology: Personal Growth to Peak Performance* (Boston, MA: McGraw-Hill), 4th edn, pp. 312–332.

Noel, R. (1980). 'The effect of visuo-motor behaviour rehearsal on tennis performance'. *Journal of Sport Psychology* 2: 221–226.

Onestak, D. (1997). 'The effect of visuo-motor behaviour rehearsal (VMBR) and videotaped modeling (VM) on the free-throw performance of intercollegiate athletes'. *Journal of Sport Behaviour* 20 (2): 185–198.

Paivio, A. (1985). 'Cognitive and motivational functions of imagery in human performance'. *Canadian Journal of Applied Sport Science* 10: 22–28.

Richardson, Alan. (1984). *The Experiential Dimension of Psychology* (Queensland, Australia: University of Queensland Press).

Rizzolatti, G., Fogassi, L. & Gallese, V. (2001). 'Neurophysiological mechanisms underlying the understanding and imitation of action'. *Nature Neuroscience Reviews* 2: 661–670.

Robin, N., Dominique, L., Toussaint, L., Blandin, Y., Guillot, A. & Le Her, M. (2007). 'Effects of motor imagery training on service return accuracy in tennis: the role of imagery ability'. *International Journal of Sport and Exercise Psychology* 5 (2): 175–188.

Rogerson, L. & Hrycaiko, D. (2002). 'Enhancing competitive performance in ice hockey goaltenders using centering and self-talk'. *Journal of Applied Sport Psychology* 14: 14–26.

Roos, H., Ornell, M., Gardsell, P., Lohmander, L. & Lindstrand, A. (1995). 'Soccer after anterior cruciate ligament injury – an incompatible combination? A national survey of incidence and risk factors and a 7-year follow-up of 310 players.' *Scandinavian Journal of Medicine and Science in Sports* 5: 107–112.

Rotella, R., Gansneder, B., Ojala, D. & Billing, J. (1980). 'Cognitions and coping strategies of elite skiers. An exploratory study of young developing athletes.' *Journal of Sport Psychology* 2: 350–354.

Rushall, B. & Lippman, L. (1998). 'The role of imagery in physical performance'. *International Journal of Sport Psychology* 29: 57–72.

Ryan, D. & Simons, J. (1982). 'Efficacy of mental imagery in enhancing mental rehearsal of motor skills'. Journal of Sport Psychology 4: 41–51.

Ryan, D. & Simons, J. (1983). 'What is learned in mental practice of motor skills'. *Journal of Sport Psychology* 5: 219–426.

Sackett, R. (1934). 'The influences of symbolic rehearsal upon the retention of a maze habit'. *Journal of General Psychology* 13: 113–128.

Sheikh, A. & Korn, E. (1994). *Imagery in Sports and Physical Performance* (Amityville, NY: Baywood).

Short, S., Bruggeman, J., Engel, S., Marback, T., Wang, L.,

Willadsen, A. & Short, M. (2002). 'The effect of imagery function and imagery direction on self-efficacy and performance on a golf-putting task'. *The Sport Psychologist* 16: 48–67.

Smith, D., Collins, D. & Holmes, P. (2003). 'Impact and mechanism of mental practice effects on strength'. *International Journal of Sport and Exercise Psychology* 1: 293–306.

Suinn, R. (1982). 'Imagery in sports'. In A. Sheikh (ed.), *Imagery, Current Theory, Research, and Application* (New York: Wiley), pp. 507–534.

Surburg, P., Porretta, D. & Sutlive, V. (1995). 'Use of imagery practice for improving a motor skill'. *Adapted Physical Activity Quarterly* 12 (3): 217–227.

Taylor, J. & Taylor, S. (1997). *Psychological Approaches to Sports Injury Rehabilitation* (Gaithersburg, MD: Aspen).

Taylor, J. & Wilson, G. (2005). *Applying Sport Psychology: Four Perspectives* (Champaign, IL: Human Kinetics).

Vadocz, E., Hall, C. & Moritz, S. (1997). 'The relationship between competitive anxiety and imagery use'. *Journal of Applied Sport Psychology* 9 (2): 241–253.

Vealey, R. & Greenleaf, C. (1998). 'Seeing is believing: Understanding and using imagery in sport'. In J. M. Williams (ed.), *Applied Sport Psychology: Personal Growth to Peak Performance* (Boston, MA: McGraw-Hill), pp. 220–224.

Weinberg, R. & Gould, D. (2006). *Foundations of Sport and Exercise Psychology* (Champaign, IL: Human Kinetics), 4th edn.

Weinberg, R., Seabourne, T. & Jackson, A. (1981). 'Effect of visuo-motor behavior rehearsal, relaxation, and imagery on karate performance'. *Journal of Sport Psychology* 10: 71–78.

White, A. & Hardy, L. (1995). 'Use of different imagery perspectives on the learning and performance of different motor skills'. *British Journal of Psychology* 86: 191–216.

Wrisberg, C. & Ragsdale, M. (1979). 'Cognitive demand and practice level: Factors in the mental rehearsal of motor skills'. *Journal of Human Movement Studies* 5: 201–208.

Zittman, F., Dyck, R., Spinhoven, P., Linssen, A. & Corrie, G. (1992). 'Hypnosis and autogenic training in the treatment of tension headaches: A two-phase constructive design study with follow-up'. *Journal of Psychosomatic Research* 36: 219–228.

http://scholar.lib.vt.edu/ejournals/JITE/v32n4/whetstone.html
https://www.psychologytoday.com/blog/flourish/200912/seeing-is-
  believing-the-power-visualization

Chapter 10
Barnes, G. M., Welte, J. W., Tidwell, M. C. & Hoffman, J. H.
  (2011). 'Gambling on the Lottery: Sociodemographic Correlates
  Across the Lifespan'. *Journal of Gambling Studies* 27 (4): 575–86.
  doi: 10.1007/s10899-010-9228-7.
http://fortune.com/2016/01/15/powerball-lottery-winners/
http://www.theghostcoders.com/799/you-just-won-a-lottery
  -10shocking-factsabout-the-lottery
http://journalistsresource.org/studies/economics/personal-finance/
  research-review-lotteries-demographics#sthash.ojrlp1te.dpuf

Chapter 11
Artherholt, S. B. & Fann, J. R. (2012). 'Psychosocial care in
  cancer'. *Current Psychiatry Reports* 14 (1): 23–29.
Bachorowski, J.-A., Smoski, M. J. & Owren, M. J. (2001). 'The
  acoustic features of human laughter'. *Journal of the Acoustical
  Society of America* 110: 1581.
Bakhtin, Mikhail (1941). *Rabelais and His World* (Bloomington:
  Indiana University Press).
Bogard, M. (2008). *Laughter and its Effects on Groups* (New
  York: Bullish Press).
Chapman, Antony J., Foot, Hugh C. & Derks, Peter (eds) (1996).
  Humor and Laughter: Theory, Research, and Applications (NJ.
  Transaction Publishers).
Cousins, Norman (1979). *Anatomy of an Illness as Perceived by
  the Patient* (New York. WW Norton).
Cousins, Norman (1983). *Anatomy of an Illness* (New York:
  Bantam Doubleday Dell).
Davila-Ross, M., Allcock, B., Thomas, C. & Bard, K. A.
  (2011). 'Aping expressions? Chimpanzees produce distinct
  laugh types when responding to laughter of others.' *Emotion*.
  Oct;11(5):1013- 20. doi:10.1037/a0022594.
Fashoyin-Aje, L. A., Martinez, K. A. & Dy, S. M. (2012). 'New
  patient-centered care standards from the Commission on Cancer:

opportunities and challenges'. *Journal of Supportive Oncology*: e-pub ahead of print 20 March 2012. http://www.ncbi.nlm.nih. gov /pubmed/22440532

Fried, I., Wilson, C. L., MacDonald, K. A. & Behnke, E. J. (1998). 'Electric current stimulates laughter'. *Nature* 391:650.

Goel, V. & Dolan, R. J. (2001). 'The functional anatomy of humor: segregating cognitive and affective components'. *Nature Neuroscience* 3: 237–238.

Greig, John Young Thomson (1923). *The Psychology of Comedy and Laughter* (New York: Dodd, Mead and Co.).

Holmes, T. H. & Rahe, R. H. (1967). 'The social readjustment rating scale'. *Journal of Psychosomatic Research* 11: 213.

Jenkins, Ron (1994). *Subversive Laughter* (New York: Free Press), pp. 13ff.

Johnson, S. (2003). 'Emotions and the Brain'. *Discover* 24 (4). discover.com

Kawakami, K., et al. (2006). 'Origins of smile and laughter: A preliminary study'. *Early Human Development* 82: 61–66. kyoto-u.ac.jp

Klein, A. (1998). *The Courage to Laugh: Humor, Hope and Healing in the Face of Death and Dying* (Los Angeles, CA: Tarcher/Putman).

Krichtafovitch, Igor (2006). *Humor Theory: The Formulae of Laughter* (Colorado: Outskitspress).

Lutgendorf, S. K., DeGeest, K., Dahmoush, L. et al. (2011). 'Social isolation is associated with elevated tumor norepinephrine in ovarian carcinoma patients'. *Brain, Behavior, and Immunity* 25 (2): 250–255.

Lutgendorf, S. K., Sood, A. K., Anderson, B. et al. (2005). 'Social support, psychological distress, and natural killer cell activity in ovarian cancer'. *Journal of Clinical Oncology* 23 (28):7105– 7113. http://www.ncbi.nlm.nih.gov/pubmed/16192594

Lutgendorf, S. K., Sood, A. K. & Antoni, M. H. (2010). 'Host factors and cancer progression: biobehavioral signaling pathways and interventions'. *Journal of Clinical Oncology* 28 (26): 4094– 4099. http://www.ncbi.nlm.nih.gov/pubmed/20644093

MacDonald, C. (2004). 'A Chuckle a Day Keeps the Doctor Away: Therapeutic Humor & Laughter'. *Journal of Psychosocial*

Nursing and Mental Health Services 42 (3):18–25. psychnurse.org

Marteinson, Peter (2006). *On the Problem of the Comic: A Philosophical Study on the Origins of Laughter* (Ottawa: Legas Press). utoronto.ca

McDonald, P. G., Antoni, M. H., Lutgendorf, S. K. et al. (2005). 'A biobehavioral perspective of tumor biology'. *Discovery Medicine* 5 (30): 520–526.

Melhem-Bertrandt, A., Chavez-Macgregor, M., Lei, X. et al. (2011). 'Beta-blocker use is associated with improved relapse-free survival in patients with triple-negative breast cancer'. *Journal of Clinical Oncology* 29 (19): 2645–2652.

Milius, S. (2001). 'Don't look now, but is that dog laughing?' *Science News* 160 (4): 55. sciencenews.org

Miller, M., Mangano, C., Park, Y., Goel, R., Plotnick, G. D. & Vogel, R. A. (2006). 'Impact of cinematic viewing on endothelial function'. *Heart* 92 (2): 261–262. doi:10.1136/hrt.2005.061424.

Moeller, Hans-Georg & Wohlfart, Günter (2010). *Laughter in Eastern and Western Philosophies* (Freiburg/Munich: Verlag Karl Alber).

Moreno-Smith, M., Lutgendorf, S. K. & Sood, A. K. (2010). 'Impact of stress on cancer metastasis'. *Future Oncology* 6 (12): 1863–1881.

Panksepp, J. & Burgdorf, J. (2003). '"Laughing" rats and the evolutionary antecedents of human joy?' *Physiology & Behavior* 79: 533–547.psych.umn.edu

Provine, R. R. (1996). 'Laughter'. *American Scientist* 84 (38): 45. ucla.edu

Raskin, Victor (1985). *Semantic Mechanisms of Humor*. (Boston: D. Reidel Publishing Company).

Riley,V. (1968). 'Role of the LDH-elevating virus in leukemia therapy by asparaginase'. *Nature* 220: 1245–1246.

Segerstrom, S. C. & Miller, G. E. (2004). 'Psychological stress and the human immune system: a meta-analytic study of 30 years of inquiry'. *Psychological Bulletin* 130 (4): 601–630.

Simonet, P., et al. (2005). 'Dog Laughter: Recorded playback reduces stress-related behavior in shelter dogs'. Seventh International Conference on Environmental Enrichment.petalk.org

Skinner, Quentin. (2004). 'Hobbes and the Classical Theory of

Laughter' (PDF). Retrieved 23 October 2006. In Sorell, Tom
  & Foisneau, Luc (2004). *Leviathan After 350 Years* (Oxford:
  Oxford University Press), pp. 139–166.
Sloan, E. K., Priceman, S. J., Cox, B. F. et al. (2010). 'The
  sympathetic nervous system induces a metastatic switch in
  primary breast cancer'. *Cancer Research* 70 (18): 7042–7052.
Spence, D. P., Scarborough, H. S. & Ginsberg, E. H. (1987).
  'Lexical correlates of cervical cancer'. *Social Science of Medicine*
  12: 141–145.
http://jdc.jefferson.edu/cgi/viewcontent.cgi?article=1108&context
  =jeffjpsychiatry
http://citeseerx.ist.psu.edu/viewdoc/download?doi=10.1.1.575
  .2841& rep=rep1&type=pdf
http://www.fertstert.org/article/S0015-0282(10)02958-4/references
http://www.themoscowtimes.com/sitemap/free/2004/3/article/patch
  -adams-prescribes-his-laughter-therapy/232329.html
http://www.psych.nyu.edu/phelpslab/whoweare.html

Chapter 12

Claparède, Édouard (1911). *Experimental Pedagogy and the
  Psychology of the Child* (University of Michigan Library).
LeDoux, Joseph (1998). *The Emotional Brain: The Mysterious
  Underpinnings of Emotional Life* (New York: Simon & Schuster).
http://www.adaa.org/finding-help